Till Death DO US PART

THE COMPLETION OF THE COVENANT

SHAMEKA BAILEY

Book Cover Design: Prize Publishing House

Printed by: Prize Publishing House, LLC in the United States of America.

First printing edition 2023.

Prize Publishing House
P.O. Box 9856, Chesapeake, VA 23321
www.PrizePublishingHouse.com

Library of Congress Control Number:2023910387

ISBN (Paperback): 979-8-9875046-8-0
ISBN (E-Book): 979-8-9875046-9-7

CONTENTS

Dedication v

Introduction vii

Chapter 1   What Is Love? 1

Chapter 2   I Chose Me. 7

Chapter 3   How It All Began 9

Chapter 4   Should I Stay Or Should I Go?. 17

Chapter 5   I Knew That He'd Be Mine 27

Chapter 6   A Forever Love 35

Chapter 7   Beyond The Veil 47

Chapter 8   I'll Always Love You 57

Chapter 9   The Importance Of Support. 71

Chapter 10   How Can I Live Without You?. 77

Chapter 11   Precious Memories 85

A Prayer For You. 97

DEDICATION

Father God, without you, I am nothing! Thank You for trusting me with this journey. Thank You for keeping me. Thank You for carrying me through.

In loving memory of my amazing husband, Walter Martez Bailey! You were "Heaven sent." Without you, this part of my story wouldn't be possible. You embodied Ephesians 5:25 and loved me just as Christ instructed you. Because of the love that you gave to me, I can now love myself. Because of your patience with me, I know that I don't have to be guarded. Because of your unconditional love, I know I'm worth fighting for. You showed me that I can be loved correctly, honored, and respected by a man. Now I know what I deserve. You've left your footprints here on earth and a permanent imprint on my heart and the hearts of everyone who knew you. You shall never be forgotten!

I thank our children, Tee and Brooke, for your strength. Thank you for bearing with me as I embarked on this journey. Thank you for being patient and understanding as I experienced many different emotions. Thank you for being my motivation and my reasons to keep on keeping on. I'm honored to be your mother.

To every widow, the Bible says in Revelation 12:11 that we are overcome by the blood of the lamb and the words of our testimony. I know this experience wasn't just for me but for you too! Let my story renew your FAITH. Know that you are LOVED! There is HOPE! You WILL make it! You shall LIVESTRONG!

INTRODUCTION

I grew up in a world without the guidance of a father. In a moment, my innocence was taken away from me. What was once valuable was now tarnished. God's promise is that "All things work for the good of them that love Him and are called according to his purpose" (Romans 8:28). No experience was ever wasted. He made all things beautiful and gave me beauty for my ashes. God allowed me to see His love given to me through something that I've never known nor seen love from…. a man. The man that chose me to be his wife. My husband.

Till death do us part. It's not just a phrase; it's a promise to stand by each other through thick and thin, sickness and health, until the end of our lives. It's a vow that says no matter what comes our way, we will face it together. Everyday won't be easy, but every moment will be worth it. We will choose to overcome every challenge and celebrate every victory. Because at the end of the day, we have each other. And that is all that truly matters. I know there will be tough times ahead, but I also know that we can get through them together. With Christ as our guide and strength from one another, there is nothing we can't conquer. We'll take on whatever comes our way.

Till death do us part. It's a phrase that carries so much weight and meaning. When we say those words to our partner in the presence of God and stand before witnesses, we're making a promise that goes beyond the physical realm. We're saying that no matter what happens, we'll stick by each other until the very end. We'll weather any storm together, whether sickness, financial struggles, or even disagreements. It's not just a promise to stay together until we die. It's a vow to support each other through life's journey, to always be there for one another, and to never give up on our relationship. Till death do us part may seem like just a few simple words, but they hold a depth of emotion and commitment that can't be expressed with any other phrase. A vow that should never be broken yet one that is only fulfilled after death.

Losing your spouse can be one of the hardest things that you will ever go through. Widowhood is a time filled with sorrow, grief, confusion, and uncertainty about what comes next. It's normal to feel lost without your partner by your side. You will feel like a part of you is missing and that life will never be the same again. You may miss their laugh or the way they used to hold your hand. You might find yourself wishing you could hear their voice just once more or see them smile again. It can be daunting to face life's challenges solo, but it's important to remember that you are strong enough to do it. What we've endured, we survived! Someone else may not have made it through. Our Heavenly Father chose us specifically for this assignment. There will be good days and bad days, moments when memories flood your mind and others where you can enjoy the present. It's okay to take your time processing your feelings and to lean on friends and family for support. Widowhood isn't something anyone chooses, but it's a reality that many will face.

Widowhood is a heart-wrenching experience. The pain of losing your spouse is inevitable. You'll feel like a part of you has been ripped away. The loneliness can be overwhelming; sometimes, it feels like the world is closing in on you. Grief comes in waves; every day can feel like an uphill battle. There are moments when you find yourself lost in memories, unable to shake off the sadness. On other days, you may feel angry or frustrated that your partner was taken from you too soon.

Widowhood also brings with it a sense of uncertainty about the future. You're left wondering how you'll manage without your spouse by your side. It's a daunting prospect, but one that you know you'll have to face head-on. Despite the pain, widowhood can also bring some unexpected blessings. You learn to cherish the moments you had with your partner and appreciate life's simple pleasures.

Ultimately, widowhood is a journey that nobody wants to take, but it's one that many will inevitably face. Although it's tough, know that you're right where God wants you to be. He has both a purpose and a plan for you.

After reading this book, I pray that you will cherish and honor these words with every moment you spend together. If your spouse has transitioned, I pray you will grieve and heal properly.

WHAT IS LOVE?

Is it just a four-letter word spoken
Just to entice someone's emotions
That four-letter word is used like a special potion
To play on your emotions
Causing you to let your guard down

What is LOVE?
Is it something that I should embrace
Meanwhile, all it does is take from me
Am I being deceived
As I blindly begin my journey

Because LOVE was never properly delivered
I have no filter
I can't decipher what's authentic and what's counterfeit
Because it all looks the same
And who's to blame
Because LOVE never lived here

WHAT IS LOVE?

A father sets the tone for how his daughter interprets love. She has no blueprint to guide her through this cold world in his absence.

As a young girl, my father meant the world to me! Every little girl desires to be the twinkle in her father's eyes. I honestly felt that way for a long time. There wasn't a thing that my father could do wrong in my eyes. I was his baby girl, and though I didn't have both of my parents in one home, as long as my daddy showed up, I was okay. I was too young to remember my parents living in the same home. Looking back through some photo albums, I can see that once upon a time, we were all together. I remember him coming home on furloughs from the halfway house and picking my brother and me up for the day. We would ride the train to 69th Street, catch a movie, and take pictures at the photo booth. It didn't matter to me that my daddy would have to leave me again. I would always try to enjoy the moment. After a while, those furlough visits vanished. The only chance to see my daddy was by visiting him in prison. My momma didn't like taking us there, so it was rare.

My daddy's incarceration lasted for the majority of my life. The streets were all that he knew. The streets gave him a place to feel loved and appreciated. The streets gave him a name. But that came with a cost. The price of being absent from my life is what he paid. Could I really blame him for the road he embarked on when someone clearly dropped the ball in his life too? My momma wasn't as gracious as me. She didn't appreciate his decisions, which left her to raise two babies alone. Still, there was nothing that she could say to sway my love for him, not that she ever tried too. I would be the one always defending him because he was my daddy!

Unfortunately, life has a way of showing you what you're missing. The absence of my father became very evident. On birthdays and holidays, I might get a phone call or even a customized card that one of his fellow inmates drew for me. That didn't quite fill the void for me, though. Occasional pep talks just weren't the same as being able to lay in my daddy's arms at night.

I was an honor roll student. I always set the bar high for myself. I never really fit in, either. So there I was, fatherless and peculiar. The guys my mom usually dated were pretty cool for as long as I can remember. She started dating a guy; he seemed charming, but he was clearly different. I watched him abuse my mom in every way. Though I didn't have a clear picture of what love was, I was very clear on what it wasn't. I knew she didn't deserve how she was being treated, but she loved him, so she stayed. Seeing how fast he'd turn into another person was pretty scary. He tried to control her every move. Most people were convinced that he was this spectacular person, but I saw the demons that arose behind closed doors. I had to protect my mother at all costs. I couldn't just stand around and watch her get hurt anymore. I would always confront him with my little self. I was fearless when it came to her. I remember being so fed up one day that I went into my grandma's kitchen and grabbed a butcher knife. Oh, I was going to kill him! I had to take him out before he really hurt my mother. I remember her screaming as my grandma tried to get the knife out of my hand. I remember the devilish look in his eyes as I stared back at him while he taunted me as if I was a joke, asking what I would do with the knife. My momma still stayed. Yet another distorted view of what love was.

Though I never really liked him, he was the only male presence in my life. The role of a father he stepped into. I had my reservations, but I had no choice but to go along with it. He clearly wasn't going anywhere. That man had a way of making you think that you were the problem. He was so cunning that he could make you believe an entire lie. I had no idea that my world was getting ready to change forever.

I'd reached one of the most significant milestones in life, PUBERTY! No more stuffing tissue in my shirt, lol. I even grew some pubic hair. I remember sharing that specific thing with my mom. That's when it all began. I had the middle room. I had no walls or even a door. There was clear access to where I was. He came to me and told me that my mom had told him about my pubic hair, and he asked me if he could see it. Of course I'm in shock! I'm eleven years old. What can I possibly do?

I knew this wasn't right, but no one was there to help me. I was told that everything was okay, as if this was normal, and not to tell my mom or anyone. It started as a touch as he would gaze at my vagina as if he was obsessed with it. He eventually asked me to "kiss it," telling me it won't hurt as he placed his fingers inside me. I would lay there helplessly, not knowing what to do. He would be at the foot of my bed every chance he could. It was worse when my mom went to work.

This man was now my mother's husband, and he was the father of my little sister. I often asked myself why me when he had four daughters of his own. *Why did my mother have to tell him about my most intimate moments? What was I supposed to do now?* Lonely and confused, I was violated in my own home by someone who was supposed to protect me. After a while, I couldn't get anything for free;

everything cost me my body. Eventually, I found myself running away, trying to escape my situation, which put me in even more compromising situations. *I must be cursed; could my life get any worse? I don't deserve this; why is this happening to me?* I found myself running from the voices in my head. I always felt like I was being chased.

As time passed, I felt worthless. Something in me believed that I deserved better. I tried to put the pieces of my life together and find some normalcy. Then one day, I found out that I was carrying my angel. Most thought that my life couldn't get any worse. I was written off, but they didn't know my baby gave me something to live for. When I had nothing left to live for, she became my reason. I could never give up now; I had to fight to live for her.

WHO AM I?

*I've found myself on a quest to find my own
identity
So much trauma and pain
But those things don't define me
I used to walk around with my head held down
I couldn't see
So that caused me to walk in circles
It wasn't until I lifted my head
That I was able to see the light that guided me into my destiny
This path that I now walk is the one that God
created for me
Finally, I've gotten a glimpse of who I am*

I CHOSE ME

The Importance Of Healing Yourself First

The things I've experienced up to this point should have IMMEDIATELY taken me out! If the enemy had his way, that's exactly what would've happened. Fortunately, I have a Heavenly Father who has always had His hand on my life. He placed greatness and purpose inside of me. Though I could never fully see what it was, I knew that it was something different about me. I never fit in. I don't care how hard I tried; it never worked. Heck, the people that I'd try to mingle with would even notice. They noticed that I was different. Something was different.

I loved school! I rarely missed a day, even during my pregnancy. I don't think anybody dreams of being a teen mom, but my daughter was the best thing that has ever happened to me. Dropping out of high school was never an option for me. I was even more motivated to accomplish my goal of graduating. I did just that! My baby girl was right there by my side. I promised myself that I would NEVER be a statistic.

I had to literally choose to separate myself from people who didn't deserve me. No longer would I settle for less than I deserve. I'd no longer compromise to have someone in my space who didn't value me. I had always known I was valuable, but I could finally walk in that truth. Yes, I was still broken, but I had decided that no one would ever have access to break me again. I chose to prioritize my happiness and get back to doing the things that I loved!

I was so focused! My goal was to create a world that was suitable for my daughter. I came across a job opportunity that would've allowed me to bring in some funds by serving underprivileged kids and their communities. It was a no-brainer for me, and I applied for the position. I had to write an essay, get referrals, and be interviewed for the position. I nailed it, of course! This position took a lot of focus, dedication, and discipline; I had no time for distractions. I was happily single and had no desire for a relationship.

I'd finally begun to live again and to create a new normal for my daughter and me. My past was no longer an anchor that weighed me down but was a steppingstone for my future endeavors. I could turn my pain into purpose and reach back to help other young mothers. I was now a beacon of light that shined on the seemingly dark paths of other young girls. They were where I used to be. I became a part of the roadmap to success for them.

I could finally enjoy the things in life that brought me happiness. My past experiences were no longer badges of shame that I had to carry. I had finally begun to heal and walk in purpose on purpose. Everything wasn't crystal clear at this point in my life, but I could definitely see a brighter future for me. It is said that once you stop looking, things will find you. Well, I'm not looking anymore.

HOW IT ALL BEGAN

Was He Really Single?

I remember this day like it was yesterday. It was my first day at my after-school work site. My team and I arrived in our bright red jackets, khaki pants, and Timberland boots, ready to work. My coworker and I were working with a group of scholars. She noticed this guy. Heck, I noticed him, too, actually! He was tall, handsome, he had an amazing smile and did I mention that he was fly!!!! Yeah, I saw all of that. I had checked him out way before she mentioned anything. There was just seemingly one potentially huge problem, though. I noticed this female who seemed to follow him everywhere he went. My coworker must have been too googly-eyed that she missed that part, but I didn't. She tried to throw me the oop (set me up), but I kindly declined and told her about my findings since she clearly had overlooked them. I said, "Girl, don't you see that female following him around like she's attached to his hip?" She said, "Girl, you think so?" with a slight chuckle. I replied, "Yes, he clearly is off limits, and that's his girlfriend." I honestly didn't know for sure. I did know one thing, though, I had absolutely no time for anybody's games. After years of selling myself short, I knew what I deserved. I wasn't really looking for a relationship anyway. I was okay with being single. It felt good to just think about me and what I needed. I'd never settle or be played again. I was focused. I was there to do my job, and that's it.

Everyone introduced themselves, and it was customary for them to call you brother or sister before your names. It took a while to get used to because the only other place that I'd used those terms was in church.

His name was Brother Walt. He practically ran the afterschool program. He loved the scholars, and they absolutely adored him! He was so patient. He was smooth yet firm in his communication with them. He never raised his voice, and sometimes all he would have to do was give them a good look. You know, the look your momma would give you when you started losing your mind, lol. Yeah, that was the look. It was such a rare sight to see. Let me tell you all, that man looked even better up close. He was FINE! His charm was out of this world. He smelled so good, and his smile was contagious. He was well-kept, and did I mention that he had all his teeth? Lol, yes, I loved his whole grill. I could tell he was checking me out too, but I knew the signs of a taken man when I saw them. I just don't have time for that!

Throughout the day, we'd do different activities with the scholars. There were certain days that they would travel to another site for specials. Today was that day. Brother Walt usually would load the scholars up in the van and take them to the site. It was requested for a couple of us to go with him and the scholars to the other site, and guess who volunteered to go? I sure did! Traveling to the site was a breeze. I could tell that the scholars were excited to go to specials. The energy in the van was on another level! They sang songs and laughed; it was just amazing! The mystery female stayed back at the original site, so I got to check him out apart from her.

When we arrived, the children participated in different activities led by the site coordinator. An activity came up, and some volunteers were needed for it. I, along with Brother Walt and two scholars, was chosen. We were given a scenario. Brother Walt was the husband, I was the wife, and the two scholars were our children. The scenario had something to do with us chastising our children. Brother Walt ended up completely running the show, and I tried to jump in, but he had it covered. There were some times when I thought that he was being too easy on our children. Yeah, we were acting, but it felt so real. After we were done, all we could do was laugh. Our chemistry just came naturally. It was almost like we had known each other forever. As we returned to our seats, Brother Walt smiled and said, "Sister Shameka, you were a good wife." I was beyond flattered. I mean, he was smiling from ear to ear. I was in a daze for a moment until I realized that I had to say something. I finally replied, "Thank you, Brother Walt. You were a good husband too."

We continued with our day at specials. The scholars had an amazing time. When it was our time to return to the afterschool site, we loaded the scholars up on the van and made our way back.

When we arrived, Brother Walt opened the double doors so the scholars could get out. I held the door while they made their way inside. After the last scholars went in, I was about to enter when Brother Walt called my name. He said, "Sister Shameka would it be ok if I asked you for your phone number?" I shot back immediately, "What do you want my number for!" The way my mind was set up then, that response just came out. I had come across so many jokers that I had to ask up front what are your intentions so that I don't waste my time. It just slipped right out, though, like it was programmed there or something. The other thing was that this man had a whole girlfriend, so why was he asking me for my phone number? I think that I scared the man half to death with my response. He stood there, both shocked and perplexed at the same time. He paused and quickly replied, "Oh,

I'm sorry I shouldn't have asked." I replied, "No, it's fine. I didn't mean it like that. It's okay." I tried to recover that fumble because it got awkward real quick! I asked him why he wanted my number if he already had a girlfriend. He said, "Who? I don't have a girlfriend." I replied, "Then who's that female that keeps following you around everywhere?" He laughed and explained that she was an older scholar who was like a junior helper. She just liked to follow him around like the other scholars. We both laughed, and I breathed a sigh of relief. I told him I didn't have time for foolishness, so I'm glad this got cleared up. He just couldn't believe that I thought that she was his girlfriend. We both went back inside and finished up the rest of the day.

When our day was over, my coworkers and I would walk up to Broad Street to get on the train. My coworker from earlier that day and I were walking and talking about the day's events. I told her he asked for my number and how I initially responded. She told me that I was crazy as she burst out laughing. Out of nowhere, we heard a horn beeping. When we turned to see who it was, it was Brother Walt. He was dropping some of the scholars off. He honked the horn as he waved at us with a big ole smile on his face. Guess who was sitting in the front passenger seat with her feet propped up? The same girl that I thought was his girlfriend, lol. My coworker and I laughed uncontrollably as we continued to make our way to the train.

I had choir rehearsal that evening. I mentioned that to Brother Walt so that he could just call me afterward. By the time I reached my destination, he had already called me and left a message. He said, "Hi, Sister Shameka, it's brother Walt. I know that you're at choir rehearsal, but I just wanted to give you a call. This is my number. Let me know when you get home safe." I honestly was so impressed. I had never had a guy reach out to me so fast and seem so caring. He knew I was busy, but he still put forth the effort to show me he was more than interested. I couldn't wait to get home so that I could call him.

After choir rehearsal, I headed home, and we eventually got on the phone. We laughed about everything that had happened earlier that day. Walt could hold a conversation about anything. He was extremely intelligent and well-spoken. He was simply AMAZING! We spent the rest of the night on the phone. We were inseparable from that day on.

When I would come to work, I was always in my uniform. My uniform was comfortable; nothing form-fitting. I had gotten so used to wearing it; I almost forgot what regular clothes were. I'd wake up, put on my uniform, come home, shower, and jump into bed. There were days that I just wanted to wear regular clothes. One day after work, I changed into my regular clothes. I had nowhere to go but home, but I was tired of wearing my uniform all the time. When Walt saw me, his mouth literally hit the floor. I was just regularly dressed in my mind. But by his reaction, he was wowed! He immediately stopped what he was doing, and I had all his attention.

I wore a brown shirt with a V-cut by the neck (it was trimmed with gold sequins), a pair of blue jeans with brown trim around the pockets, and my favorite brown boots. He exclaimed, "Hold up, where are you going?" I laughed and replied, "Nowhere but home." He said, "Ain't no way you're looking this good and going straight home." I replied, "I'm tired of wearing my uniform; these are regular clothes to me." This was another good sign for me. He noticed me. He paid attention to me. He could affirm me like no other, and I loved it!

My job at the time only required that we go to the afterschool program a few days out of the week. So there were times when I didn't get to see Walt every day. Regardless, we talked everyday! At that time, Walt went to Community College during the day, and I worked at a neighboring high school. We would meet for lunch every day. It got to the point where my coworkers already knew my plans for the day. They saw our love blooming. But we were just friends. If I couldn't make it out to lunch, he'd bring it to me. Though I promised myself I'd take my time, he made the chance at love again worth taking. He was a true friend.

As time passed, there wasn't anything that I wouldn't do for Walt. At one point, the staff was low at the afterschool site. He was frustrated, and I could tell. I'd tell my coworkers I was leaving our site early just to go and help him. I never liked to see him frustrated. Besides, he was such a gentle giant that screaming or using foul language didn't make sense. It wasn't his character, so it was kind of funny when he'd be in the moment. Not that I would laugh at him. It was just not his character at all.

He made coming to work worth it. I could always depend on him to make my day better. Walt was just that kind of guy. I loved my afterschool program! I built such a strong bond with the scholars. I was honored to be one of their cheerleaders, someone who would support them and ensure they would succeed!

When the public schools were closed, my team and I would go to the afterschool program for the entire day. There was so much for the children to do -guest speakers, special events, arts and crafts, book clubs, etc. It was never a dull moment there.

Walt and I just clicked. We both loved children. We both worked in the field. We both had patience with them that money couldn't buy (we were born with that gift). Our purposes were aligned. It felt good to have someone who could relate to me.

Outside of Walt, Brother Anya was my favorite person at the afterschool program. He played an intricate part in our relationship. He saw the googly eyes and our yard-long smiles when we were together. He'd tease us and tell us that we'd be together. He'd say that we were going to get married one day. Though our chemistry was inevitable, it was obvious. We'd both deny his claims because we were just friends.

At the afterschool site, they had a "No Scrambling" rule. That meant that guys and girls weren't supposed to mingle at all relationally. We weren't even supposed to look like we were together at work. Walt and I had grown so close that staying too far away from each other became hard. At certain points during the day, we would sneak off into the kitchen or to an area where nobody could see us and hug each other. His hugs were AMAZING! I could've laid in his arms all day long. We planned precisely when we'd sneak off just so that we could hug each other. We'd make it back separately and just in enough time so nobody would notice we were missing.

Walt was such a giver. He'd give without expecting anything in return. He never had a motive. We often went on lunch dates, and he would always pay for it. On our first official date, we went to the movies. He bought the tickets, and when we arrived at the concession stand, I stepped up to pay for our snacks. Walt was in shock. He kept asking me if I was sure. I was not changing my mind because he always would pay. I wanted to do something for him. That seemingly small gesture blew his mind. He was so floored at my gesture. Before me, he was just used to people taking from him. I couldn't believe that as good of a man as he was, he was taken advantage of and not valued. Walt was a gem, and I was going to ensure he got everything he deserved!

4

SHOULD I STAY OR SHOULD I GO?

Walt and I were inseparable. Not a day went by that we didn't talk on the phone. It was rare that we didn't see each other. Through his actions, he had made it clear that I was a priority in his world. We spent so much time together that there wasn't any room for anyone else. Everything was perfect. Walt was my best friend. One day after work, Walt walked me to the train station. He rode with me to City Hall. None of this was out of the ordinary. As we waited for my trolley, he grabbed my hand and told me that he had to tell me something.

I was a little stuck. *What could he possibly have to say to me? What is about to happen?* I thought to myself. I could tell it was something serious because his body language suddenly shifted, and he held his head down. He looked up at me and told me how much he cared about me and never wanted to hurt me. He made it clear that hurting me was never his intention. He took a deep breath, and then he spoke. He said, "Meka, I have a girlfriend." My heart immediately sank as tears began to fill my eyes. Our perfect little world was shattered in an instant.

How could this even be possible? Why would he lead me to believe it was just us when it wasn't? How did I not see this coming? So many thoughts and emotions went running through my mind. I was crushed. My heart was broken. I was speechless. I loved this man too much to act out of character. I'd never speak things I didn't mean, even in heated moments. My only option was to quietly and quickly distance myself from him. He cried out to me as I turned and began walking away. He pleaded with me telling me that he was sorry. He had one of his moments where he'd use foul language, which felt abnormal. This time he grunted, and in anguish, he said, "Meka, I fucked up." There was nothing that he could've said to take the sting out of what he had just told me. My trolley eventually came. I watched through the window as Walt walked away in defeat.

In my mind, it was over. I told my mom what had happened; surprisingly, she wasn't even moved. It was like she was on his side. She absolutely adored Walt. He was the only guy that I dated that she called "Son." She made me feel like I was overreacting.

Walt was very persistent. He called me non-stop. I wouldn't answer, though. He'd leave me voice messages and texts; I still didn't respond. It was just too much for me to internalize at the moment. To me, it just didn't make sense. *How could this man be so different from the other men I've dated, I mean entirely, but yet have a very familiar issue?* I didn't want to deal with it. I didn't know how to. I hadn't spoken to Walt in a few days. When suddenly, there was a knock at the door. It was Walt. I couldn't believe he had the audacity to show up to my house. Not only did he show up, my mom let him in with open arms. She said, "What's up, son?" as he followed her towards the kitchen. He had to walk past me first, so he stopped to say hello.

Before I could say anything, he handed me an envelope. He said, "Meka, I understand if you don't ever want to see me again, you have every right to, but please read the letter and write me back." I took the envelope and went out to the porch just to be alone for a minute. He stayed inside with my mom. Walt was an artist. The envelope was designed with my initials on it. On the back of the envelope, he wrote, "Please don't be mad! I'm not Ne-Yo; I like when ur happy!"

I opened the letter, and it said:

> *Here's the truth. Yes, I sorta kinda have a girlfriend. No, I am not happy. No, I am no longer in love with her, but no, I do not know how to close that chapter as of right now. Lately, I see her but think of you constantly. I must admit, just in case you didn't already know, I am just a fucking retard!! I mean, you are, by far, everything that a man with sense would hope and pray for. Beautiful, smart, saved, funny, caring, loving, an amazing mother, and moreover, an amazing woman of God! All this for me, and I continue to fuck up?! How dare I?! You know what? I would completely understand if you had no more rap for me, honestly. I deserve it. I deserve it all. But I need you to know a few things first. I NEVER, NEVER, NEVER meant to hurt you. I was honest, but I wasn't always straightforward with you. And for that, I apologize. By me not trying to be another statistic in your life, I only put myself further into that category. You know, at one point, I thought that we would be just friends and talk, but I slowly came to the realization that God placed us in each other's lives. What's meant to be will be, but when it's from God, it's inevitable. Every time I thought that we would be nothing more than friends, God revealed to me something else about you that put you at the*

forefront of my mind. I can't really explain it. Like before we met, I figured I wouldn't talk to a girl that has a child because it would be a big responsibility. But honestly, since the day I met T, I have a special place in my heart for her. I love that little girl with everything in me. It's to the point now where I would be willing to fill the space of a father figure that her birth father left dormant. The way I see it, with a woman as thorough as you, whatever you bring to the table, I'll meet you halfway, at least if nothing more. You deserve that! My thoughts, hopes, and prayers for you have grown stronger and stronger within the past couple of months. What more can I say? Meka, I love you!! I know that those feelings may not be mutual, but that's honestly how I feel from the heart. Trust me; I want to be your man. I want to be your one and only, but I have to do this right and in order. So please, bear with me as I get delivered from my hypothetical trek through Egypt to get to my promised land with you. It would truly be a blessing beyond the one that you already are.

I love you 😊
-Walt XOXOXOXO

PS Write back, or if possible, talk to me. pleeeeeeeaaaase!!

As I read his five-page letter, tears began to roll down my face. I was finally able to breathe. I was relieved. He wasn't like the others. He was different, just like I had thought he was. He wasn't trying to play with my heart either, and it showed. He didn't just walk away; he fought for me. He risked it all by coming to my house unannounced, but that's because he couldn't just let me go that easy. He made it his business to make sure that I understood what was going on while at the same time conveying his feelings for me. Most importantly, he loved me just as much as I loved him. That was real love. I gathered myself, and before Walt left that night, we hugged just like we'd always done before. I know for sure that he was relieved. He hugged me like he never wanted to let me go again.

Though I had never said it out loud, my love for him was just as big as his was for me. This only confirmed what I had already felt. We slowly began to get back into our rhythm, and I wrote him back seven days later.

My letter said:

> *I know that it took me a while to get this letter to-gether, but just know that how I feel is sincere. I've never felt this way and actually felt that it was real! I love you! Don't you ever forget that. You make me smile. You dry the tears from my eyes. You show me that you care. When you're around, I feel so secure. My feelings for you, I can't ignore. I'm willing to endure everything with you.*

Poetry is how I learned to express myself growing up. I am a poet, so in true poetic fashion, I had to grace him with three of them. I wrote the first on the day after I received his letter. This poem was called "Speechless."

SPEECHLESS

Right now, I'm speechless
What can I say
I've never met a man
So sincere in all of his ways
Someone whom I've grown closer to each day
Right now, all that I can say
Is that I never want you to go away
Always stay with me by my side
My feelings for you I can no longer hide
I'm speechless right now
I don't know what to say
But what I do know is that
I never want these feelings to go away

I even hit him with the name acronyms:

Willing, Wonderful
All I want in a man, Accountable
Loving
Trustworthy, True
Energetic, Encouraging
Respectful, Responsible

The next poem was called "One Day."

ONE DAY

One day we'll be a family
There is no other man for me
I prayed and cried for this day to come true
Never knowing that it would be you
What a mighty God we serve
He preserved our relationship
Knowing that one day
We would be together forever
Nothing will separate us
Loving you is a must
No other man whom I trust
With my whole heart
Feeling for you from the start
Now here's to our new start
When we'll never be apart
Two hearts and one beat
Together who can beat us
Oh, and don't forget we both have JESUS
All that and more
ONE DAY

Lastly this poem was called "I Trust."

I TRUST

I'll trust that you'll be by my side
Someone on whom I can rely
On at all times
I trust that you will be with me
ONLY
And nothing or no one can come between us
I trust you enough
To open myself up
My heart is now in your hands
Handle it with care
Because it's fragile
And it bruises easily
But I trust that you will be gentle
I trust you enough to express my feelings
With a mindset of forever
Through any weather
I trust that you'll keep me safe
I can relate to you
I love you, I trust you
I wanna be one with you
Trust this
It's sincere
I always want you near
Forever be there
To show me that you love and care
For Tee& me

I trust you
Always and 4eva
Shameka

Clearly, from my letter, you can see that I was all in my feelings. I wrapped five pictures of Tee and me inside the letter. I tried my best to decorate his as he did mine. I wrote his initials "W.M.B" on the front with a star and the words "The only one for me" with a smiley face.

I undoubtedly was in love with Walter, and he was in love with me. His mistake didn't alter my love for him. I chose to stand by him. This love was worth fighting for.

SMH!

Please don't be mad! I'm not Ne-Yo, I like when ur happy!

W. M. B.

The only one for me ♪♫

5

I KNEW THAT HE'D BE MINE

I had never experienced a love like Walt's. It was selfless. It was caring. It was compassionate. It was heartfelt. It was genuine, amongst other things. Our friendship had blossomed to another level. Walt was my best friend. Work wasn't work at all when we were together. Things just flowed. He was so attentive to my needs, and I rarely even had to ask. He was such a gentleman. I had never experienced anyone like him. After long hours at work, he would walk with me to the train station, take the train with me to the trolley station, then take the trolley with me to 58th Street. Finally, he'd walk me home. He always made sure that I was safe.

He lived in North Philly close to 33rd and Diamond, and I lived all the way on the other side in Southwest Philly right off of 58th and Chester Ave. It didn't matter to him that he'd have to take that long ride back home. He wasn't satisfied until he saw me walk through my front door. Now that's love! Unlike before, it cost me nothing. He gave it to me freely and in abundance. Our traveling adventures on public transportation didn't last too long. Walt had purchased his first car. It was a small little white car, but it served its purpose. I was struggling to get my permit at the time, but he'd let me drive anyway. I was in shock the first time that he handed me his car keys. I initially said, "No, thank you," and "Are you sure?" But he would insist. So I'd drive. Carefully. Very carefully, lol.

I could talk to Walt about anything. I told him things that I had never shared with anyone else. One night I called him, and I was upset. I began telling him what was happening, and I wept uncontrollably. He asked if I needed him to come over. It was the middle of the night, but it didn't matter. He drove all the way to my house just to be with me. I cried on his shoulder while he reassured me everything would be okay. Then we went to our happy place, Checkers, for food and enjoyed each other's presence for the rest of the night.

Usually, his grandma would call to check up on him. Eventually, she went from, "Boy, where you at?" to "Okay, you're at Shameka's." She loved her grandson so much.

Summertime was quickly approaching, and the after-school program transitioned into another program during the summer. My job was coming to a close too, so I was looking for new employment. Walt suggested that I apply for the Summer program. I initially wasn't sold because the requirements seemed over the top. I wasn't sure if I could give what was required. Walt didn't take no for an answer, though. He would always push me beyond my limits. So, I applied. Unfortunately, my application was denied because the director didn't think I had what it took to fulfill the role needed for the program. When I delivered the news to Walt, he immediately transformed into the Incredible Hulk! He was beyond furious! I was nervous for anyone who had to encounter him at that moment because he wasn't having it. How could someone disqualify me? Walt went and addressed the matter. By the time he returned, the decision not to accept my application was reversed! I got the job! Walt fought for me. Nobody had ever fought for me like that. I knew beyond a shadow of a doubt that I was safe with him. Both physically and spiritually, he covered me.

On June 16, 2006, I graduated from my program. The celebration was held at the Marina in Penns Landing. The venue was beautiful. As usual, Walt showed up full of energy and excitement, toting balloons, gifts, and flowers. He was one of my biggest supporters. I could hear him yelling my name in the crowd like a parent at their child's graduation.

The summer program required intense training. We spent a week at the University of Maryland at Eastern Shore (UMES). I took the bus there with the others. Walt was going to meet us up there. Though he had officially broken things off with his ex, he told her he would still go to the prom with her. Walt was a man of his word, so he honored that. I had no problem with it because that decision was made before I came into the picture. Once we arrived, I got settled in my dorm room. I had lunch, and I participated in some activities. After that, I went back to my room. That evening I received a call from Walt. I was surprised because he should have been enjoying himself at the prom. He wasn't, though. Walt had actually snuck off to the bathroom to call me. I was taken aback, and I asked him why he did that. He replied that he didn't want to be there and he missed me. He's with her, but all he can think about is me. I was really missing him too, and I couldn't wait to see him the next day.

When Walt arrived, I didn't see him immediately because he was an intern and had major responsibilities. He had to assist with the activities for the day. I was the new kid on the block, so I was just a participant there to learn. Daily we'd have breakfast, lunch, and dinner. The majority of the time, Walt would miss breakfast and sometimes lunch. But that was okay because I'd gathered everything he liked throughout the day so that when I saw him at dinner, he also had breakfast and lunch. He would eat it all too. He was initially shocked that I would do such a thing, and so was everybody else because I would wrap it up and carry it with me all day. He deserved it, though. He was a hard worker, and sometimes he didn't eat. I had him covered, though. Those closest to us knew of our strong bond, but just like the rules at the afterschool program, the "No Scrambling" law was very much in effect. So we had to move accordingly. One day my mom called me, barely saying hi to me. She immediately asked where her son was at. While smiling from ear to ear, I told her that my husband was working. Walt and I were still friends, very close friends, but I knew that he was mine.

This training experience was like no other. I had never experienced anything like it. The training was so thorough that by the time I had to prepare my classroom, I was fully equipped and knew exactly what to do. This job required an energy level of 1,000! My personality is pretty reserved. I sit back and peep the scene before I jump in. I'm not really a loud person, though I love to laugh and crack jokes. One night we had a talent show, and my group was up to perform. I had to get into character, and Walt watched me from the audience. My group started to perform, and I busted out rapping and dancing. The crowd went wild, and I could see the excitement on Walt's face. He'd never seen me like this, heck I'd never seen myself like this! That night, I tapped into another side of me, and I loved it! Walt was so hyped when I came back to my seat. He said, "I ain't know that you had all of that in you." He was happy. He got to see me in his element, doing something he loved to do, and now I loved it too.

Our schedules were jam-packed during the day, so we'd barely get to see each other. It was like a breath of fresh air when we finally did. Something went wrong in my building, so we had to move to another building. As always, Walt was right there to help. Initially, I went to grab my bags, but he took them from me. He did something else that completely blew my mind. He took his hat off his head and then put it on my head. Oh, how the butterflies began to flutter. I could feel my heart beating out of my chest, and my eyes just looked at him in awe. He was so smooth, though. He just looked at me, took it all in, and smiled. I was in HEAVEN. Back then, you knew he was yours, and you were his if you got to wear his hat. The game was over for real now, lol. He walked me to my new room, we hugged, and I got settled in.

Part of our training involved creating a song for our scholars to sing in the mornings. We also had to create lesson plans and teach them to a group of seasoned interns who would then grade us on them. Our leaders would allow us time to prepare. This process was intense! I am creative and write poetry, so formulating the song was easy. Being a creative, sometimes I can have everything locked up in my head and getting it to come out is the hard part. I found myself getting beyond frustrated at times. But guess who was right there? Walt was. At the end of his long day, he would meet up with me and help me. He made sure that I was successful. He made the process easy. I couldn't draw at all, but he could. So, he'd draw the stuff, and I'd color it in! He'd stay up all night with me without once complaining. One particular night we walked quietly to the elevator, and while waiting there, our eyes met. It was one of those blush immediately; put your head down a little and squeal whaaaaaaat moments. The way that Walt would stare at me, it made me melt. I was just ready for him to kiss me at that point. The kiss didn't happen that night, though. The elevator door opened, we hugged each other like we didn't want to let each other go, and we said our good nights.

Presentation day came and went fast. I was relieved that it was finally over. It was finally time to go home. We were excited that we'd finally just be able to chill together for the ride back. That almost didn't go as planned because someone in charge tried implementing the "No Scrambling" rule on the bus. If that went into effect, the guys and the girls would have to be separated. Almost everybody bucked against that motion. We all were successful too. I took the inside seat while Walt sat in the aisle seat. We made eyes with another scrambled couple sitting together on the side of us and smiled. We were at least three hours away from home. We talked a little, laughed a little, and snored a little, lol. Suddenly Walt made another move. This move involved his handy dandy hat again. We were already sitting beside each other, which was good enough for me. But Walt went in for the kill! We couldn't be seen visibly holding hands, so when Walt grabbed my hand to hold it, he put his hat on top of our hands. This man was a GENIUS! I was officially the luckiest girl in the world! I had his hat, his hand, and most importantly, his heart. He held my hand that entire night. During the car ride home, his mom chuckled at how cute it was for us to hold hands. I already knew that he was mine, but he made it official that night. Walt never stopped holding my hand. This training experience went down as a pivotal time in our relationship. It brought us closer than ever before.

One night before Walt left my house, I walked him to the door. As I stood in the doorway, he said, "Shameka, can I kiss you?" Of course, I said yes! The coast was clear, and none of my neighbors were watching. He got closer to me and leaned in. Our lips met, and we just stayed there for a few seconds. Walt was such a character, so once we pulled away from each other, he shouted, "WOW!" Right after he had his moment, he asked for another one. Of course, I agreed. After we kissed, he told me how much he wanted to kiss me that night by the elevator when we were at training. I asked him why didn't he. I wanted him to! We had both been feeling the same way all along. Our first kiss was so special. It was so pure. I felt his love for me. I never wanted this to go away.

FOREVER IS A LONGTIME

That's how long I'll love you
There's not a thing that you could do
To change my mind
Not even the amount of times that you work my nerves
Would ever make me curve you
Because my love for you is not on a contingency plan
It's not based on whether you're right or wrong
Neither if you are weak or strong
My love for you is not a magic trick
It doesn't disappear when we don't get along
Those things just make my love for you stronger
I know that I might sound crazy
But love is not what you think
Love isn't just a smile or a bubbly feeling
Love brings out issues that need dealing
With
Can you stand the rain is the question
Because your love will be tested
Will you stay or just throw away
everything you've invested
All I know is that my love only
flourishes with you in it
So let's win together, my love

A FOREVER LOVE

Marriage was in our future. I don't think we realized how close we were to it, though. We'd talk about it on numerous occasions, and of course, that was our goal. One day my mom brought up the idea of us getting married along with her and her significant other (at that time) in a double wedding. It was an interesting idea. Something unheard of. We were young and didn't have huge bank accounts, so this would also cut the cost of what a wedding would typically cost. The year was 2006, and the following year was 2007. My mom brought up the idea of us getting married on 7/7/07. This day had a huge significance to her as a believer in Christ. God completed his creation in seven days. So this date would signify the completion of our relationship in marriage.

Some might ask why we would want to share our special day with someone else, but not only would we be making history, we'd finally be complete as one. This idea was a no-brainer for us. Walt and I began to go and look for our rings. We wanted to make sure that we got what each other liked. Neither one of us had any clue as to when the other would purchase their ring.

Walt was beyond ecstatic! It wasn't long after he purchased my ring that he was trying to propose to me. One night I was sitting on the couch in the living room, and he was like I have something for you. He was acting so weird. Pacing back and forth. I could tell that he was nervous. Before he acted like he was going to get on his knees, I asked, "Walt, what are you doing?" He was so excited that he was going to propose to me that night while I was sitting in my living room with a ring that wasn't even sized for my finger yet. I couldn't help but smile and laugh at the same time. I told him it was okay to wait until he got the ring sized. Then he could propose to me. He was just ready!

Walt and I had this thing that we'd do. We would always try to outdo each other. Everyday we'd compete to out-love each other. Things turned up a little around birthdays and special occasions. I'll admit that he just could never top me, though he never missed a beat. He put in just as much effort to ensure I always felt special.

It was Mother's Day, and every occasion was big for us! It was Walt and Tee's turn to surprise me. Everything seemed normal. Though Tee almost gave it away because she just had the giggles. My favorite restaurant at the time was Olive Garden. He drove me to the one on 15th Street. We parked, but I wasn't allowed to go inside. I had to wait in the car. This was odd. For sure, they were up to something! I couldn't put my finger on it at that moment. So I just waited with anticipation. They returned to get me, and he blindfolded me so I couldn't see. He guided me as we walked through the restaurant to our table. When we arrived, he took the blindfold off. He had flowers and balloons waiting there for me. Tee was sitting there with a big chessman cat smile full of excitement. We placed our orders, and before I knew it, Walt sprung up out of his seat, walked over to me, got down on his knees, and said, "Shameka, will you marry me?" I was completely in shock, and I screamed, "YES!" As he placed the ring on my finger, everyone in the restaurant went wild. Everyone yelled, "CONGRATULATIONS!"

It was official! We were ENGAGED! I felt like I had waited forever for this moment. But it was so worth it! I was going to marry the man of my dreams, and I couldn't have been happier. After dinner, we returned to my nana's house and showed her my ring. She joyfully exclaimed, "Oh, you did it!" She loved Walt. She knew that he would treat me right. She knew that he was a great man.

We also went over to Walt's grandma's house. She loved me, and I loved her too. She was so excited for us! I told his mom how everything happened, and she said, "I believe you" because Walt had shown her my ring, and he was beyond excited! So basically, everybody knew but kept it from me.

Marriage counseling was a must! Walt and I had the honor of having three marriage counselors. A seasoned married couple, the Goldsboroughs, and my Pastor and grandmother, the late Doris Rorie Phenix. Mrs. Goldsborough was also my seamstress, and she created my wedding dress.

On our first day of marriage counseling with my Grandma Phenix, we met at her house and sat at her table. She gave each of us a workbook, a pen, and a big yellow notepad. She began to explain what premarital counseling was and the goals and benefits of it.

Here's a glimpse at some of the questions and our responses.

One of the first questions was, "What are your expectations for premarital counseling?" Walt's response was, "My expectation of premarital counseling is to expand my knowledge on exactly what marriage is." Not surprisingly, my answer was very similar. "I expect premarital counseling to help me to understand more about marriage and to give me a better understanding of my partner."

Why would our marriage be different? Why won't it end in divorce?

Walt's response: Our marriage won't end in divorce because:

1. Other people's suggestions have no place in my marriage.
2. God has something special for us as a couple.
3. Even through the trials and tribulations, no matter how stubborn we are (I am), we learn from each other.
4. We both have JESUS!
5. We are doing things (b+b) (by the book (Bible))
6. We are us.
7. Last but not least, I love her!

My response: My marriage will be different because I have come to know my mate. I love him as a person. It took time for us to finally come together. He knows how to treat me and how to make me laugh. We also have been honest with each other. We have built up a bunch of trust. Also, we have both saved ourselves for marriage. Before we take our vows before God, we will have an understanding of what marriage is, and we will have prepared through counseling, etc. It will be both of our decisions to make.

Make a list of ten indications as to why this is the time of your life to marry.

Walt's response:

1. I sat down and told myself, if she has every quality you look for in a woman, why keep searching? There she is.
2. I am at a time in my life when I'm ready to make permanent life decisions. You shouldn't do them alone.
3. I want kids.
4. I've finally found a mate who has a heart as big as mine. Didn't think she existed.

5. I am finally ready to truly make love, not just have sex. Plus, she's actually re-saving her temple just for me and only me to enter. I'm ready to be the king of her throne.
6. We share the same family values.
7. She challenges me to be better.
8. We have strengths for each other's weaknesses.
9. I really love this woman!
10. I can become stronger in Christ with her in my life.

My response:

1. I'm in love with him.
2. He's my best friend.
3. He treats me like a Queen.
4. He is a great father to our daughter.
5. He knows how to make me laugh and comfort me.
6. Not a day goes by without me thinking about him.
7. He deals with my stubbornness.
8. He encourages me and builds me up.
9. I can talk to him about anything.
10. He is a gentleman.
11. He interacts with my daughter like no other. She loves him.
12. We complete each other.

In your relationship, what are the things you do to present yourself as a gift?

Walt's response: I surprise my mate often as a gift does most folks. Also, I'm saving my body for her to do as she pleases. I groom regularly so she finds me appealing, and I wear clothes that appeal mostly to her.

My response: I keep myself clean; how I dress is presentable. I also keep my hair done. I ask him what he likes, and I wear it. I get my nails and feet done.

What are two gift-like qualities of your future spouse?

Walt's response:

1. Her heart is all mine, and her kisses are Heavensent.
2. The way that she dresses lets me know that she wants to keep my attention.

My response:

1. I love how he deals with my child.
2. I love when he gets all fresh.

How do you know when you're in love?

Walt's response: When no matter how mad you are, you still muster up the strength to say, "I love you." When harmless words out of another's mouth hurt bad out of the mouth that you love. When you can visualize every face that person makes. When you go to sleep and wake up with a thought of them.

My response: I know that I am in love because I feel things that I've never felt before. I can't keep him off of my mind. Even when he works my nerves, I always want him around. No other man appeals to me anymore. I don't feel safe unless he's around. He knows how to comfort me in stressful situations. He completes me.

Describe the type of love that you have for one another.

Walt's response: It started out as just respect. I respected her as a woman. She was working, going to school, and was a mother. Sort of reminded me of my mom when I was younger. Just going, single and putting her thing down. Then friendship took place. I had to get to know her better, plus small sparks were present. We were hanging out and we clicked like no other female friend I ever had. Then the dramatic change after our falling out. I truly realized just how much she cared for me. So, during this phase is when my feelings developed. I had a girlfriend, but Meka was all I thought about.

My response: I have a love that started as a friendship love. As friends, we had a lot of ups and downs. I got to learn of him as a friend. Long nights on the phone, walks to the bus stop, and a skit with him as my partner (husband) all turned into a strong bond. A bond that I never desired to let go of. A bond that grew and got stronger. A strong foundation as friends now has turned into an untouchable, unbreakable love for each other that only grows stronger and deeper each day.

List the three best acts of friendship your future spouse has done for you.

Walt's response:

1. Took me back in after falling out.
2. Training (everything about it).
3. Brought his tire.

My response:

1. He's giving (training).
2. He's a good listener.
3. He knows how to make me laugh. He knows my likes/dislikes.

When you make a commitment as you take your marriage vows, what will that commitment mean to you personally?

Walt's response: My commitment to my wife means I will love, respect, and be honest and loyal to her no matter what. It is truly saying that I will love her unconditionally.

My response: This is what commitment means to me. To cherish and to hold. In each and every commitment, there are always ups and downs. When being committed to someone who is imperfect, I expect him to make mistakes. Mistakes that we can learn from, talk about and even look back on down the road and laugh about. A commitment to me is forever binding and something that lasts forever.

Is a marriage commitment to God different from a marriage commitment to your spouse?

Walt's response: The only difference is that God comes absolutely first. God gave me my wife, so appreciation and love for God first keeps my love for my wife consistent. I honor, love, and respect both, but only through God can I truly love my wife.

My response: No, because God is my first true love. In order to be committed to anyone, I have to be committed to Him first. I am made in God's image. I am given to my husband to be his helpmate. Just as I am placed on this earth to be a servant of God (God's helpmate).

What do you expect from your spouse after you are married?

Walt's response: I expect my wife to honor and understand me. I expect her to allow me to make decisions and respect them. I expect my wife to love me forever. I expect my wife to be my helpmate, my support system, my holding hand, my caretaker, my best friend, lover, and mother of my children.

My response: I expect him to be the head of the house, the provider, the example, and the protector. I expect him to love and appreciate me. I expect him to be my helpmate, my support system, my companion, my best friend.

By the time our sessions had ended, it was quite obvious that we really wanted this. Grandma Phenix saw a glow on me. She loved that Walt's love for me was authentic because that's what I deserved. However, she'd remind him that I was her grandbaby and that he better treat me right.

Time was moving fast! My dress was finally complete. Final fittings had taken place. There was one more wedding rehearsal before our big day. The newspaper even interviewed my mom and me. There was so much excitement surrounding our wedding.

Our big day had finally arrived! I hadn't seen Walt since the day before. I couldn't wait to see him. My mother, my bridal party, and I made our way into the church library, where we all got dressed. Tee and I had gotten our hair done the day before, but I didn't have a glam squad. I didn't have a makeup artist. My cousin used what she had to spruce up my face. None of that really mattered to me, though; I was just ready to marry my king! I did, in fact, purchase some contacts so I didn't have to wear my glasses. We were finally dressed, and my girls helped me put my shoes on. My veil was so beautiful. It was attached to a crown, and it was beaded all around. My dress had a sweetheart neckline trimmed in a red-colored flowered lace. The dress was off-white, so the red accents brought it all together. The back of my dress had a silver corset. The red lace was placed throughout my dress and along the bottom of it. My shoes were all red with bling straps.

My mom and I shared a special moment in the hallway before we began to make our way downstairs. My mom went first. As I waited for my sign to go, I felt my nerves begin to kick in. At that moment, I realized that this was really happening. I was calm until this point. It was my turn to go. I held my grandfather's arm as the door started to open. Everyone was standing and smiling. I was in awe as I stood at the door after they had opened it. I could only focus on my husband-to-be. He was so handsome! He had on an off-white/creamish-colored, three-piece suit. His shoes matched his attire, and he had a boutonniere pinned to his jacket with red accents. His hair was freshly cut; *Lord knows how I felt when he'd get his haircut!* He stood there with the biggest smile on his face. I had my handkerchief ready but made it to the altar without messing up my makeup.

Our ceremony was a little different. We not only had our guests with their cameras out, but the news reporters that did our interview were there taking pictures too. The things usually done once in a wedding ceremony were done twice. Instead of one, we had three wedding officiants.

One of my favorite parts of our wedding was our daughter's dedication. Walter was Tee's father. He was her best friend. He was her partner in crime. He gave her the opportunity that every little girl should have. He successfully filled the vacancy. In this part of our ceremony, he once again made the public declaration that she was his and that he would rear her as such. Walt even gave her her own ring. As the ceremony continued, we exchanged rings and lit the unity candles. We were supposed to write our own vows, but planning our wedding had gotten so overwhelming we just were ready to do it. We also took communion.

It was finally the moment that we've all been waiting for. The moment when my husband got to kiss his bride! I was so ready! Once he lifted my veil, I wrapped my arms around his head and laid it on him! His best man couldn't help but to put his head down while smiling in the background. I was officially "Mrs. Walter Martez Bailey!" We made our way into the fellowship hall to cut our beautiful three-tiered cake. We both had a small personal cake to save for our one-year anniversary. It was only right that I'd smash some cake into Walt's face. He saw it coming and gave me a look, but that didn't matter. I got him just a little on his nose. He told me that I had to lick it off and proceeded to put his nose in my face. The photographer was able to catch that special moment.

There was so much going on that we didn't even get to eat our food. We were just excited to be married. We no longer had to hear the murmurs about us being together and not married. They could just "kiss our rings" and no longer run their mouths about us because we were married.

Walt and I didn't have a honeymoon. We were actually saving up for our place. Walt also had to return to work soon. We didn't let any of that affect our moment. We were like two kids in a candy store. We were young and in love and excited to start our lives together. We went to a themed hotel located in New Jersey. It was so beautiful. We spent our first night in a love-themed suite. It had a heart-shaped jacuzzi in it. We stayed in a jungle-themed room for the remainder of our stay. We genuinely enjoyed each other. It didn't matter where we were as long as we were together.

MARRIAGE TAKES WORK

Now that the wedding is over
The real work begins
I'm so glad that we started out as friends
The foundation has been set for us to win
But we still have work to do
Our mindsets must shift
Christ must be the glue
Some days we might not like each other
But there's one thing for sure
There's not another man that I love more
I'm willing to endure with you
No one can take your place
We must never allow the space
For that to even be an option
Together we shall win

BEYOND THE VEIL

Many people focus on the wedding but have no idea what marriage truly is. The size of your ring doesn't determine the greatness of your marriage. Marriage is not that sweetheart dress with a long veil. Nor is it the three-piece custom tux. Marriage goes far beyond the wedding day. Marriage starts right after you say, "I do." Marriage takes work, and without work, your marriage won't last. A successful marriage involves continuous learning of each other. Being married doesn't make everything go away. Marriage actually exposes you. Everything that you are is now subject to the other person. There's no more hiding. Love goes from a word that brings googly eyes and butterflies to choosing to stay with that person, looking beyond their flaws. Marriage is one hell of a fight; it takes two people who want it to get in the ring and fight for it.

Walt was the kind of man that liked to fix things immediately. He prided himself on us not going to bed angry. Though his intentions were pure, I wasn't wired that way. When I was upset, I couldn't tackle the matter right away. I needed some time to digress. So when we had moments of heated fellowship, and he would try to repair things right away, I'd create an invisible fortress around myself. I'd completely block him out because I would interpret his pursuit of happiness as an attack. I wasn't used to that kind of love.

I was officially a married woman. Though I loved my husband beyond life itself, I still had my issues. I was a broken young woman (still under repair). Before him, I had gotten used to taking care of myself. Before him, every other man took from me. I was well aware that Walt wasn't like them but, in reality, the residue was still there. There were times when I didn't want to listen. There were times when I would shut completely down. I didn't fully understand what submission was, and in my ignorance, I would interpret it as him trying to tell me what to do.

Because of what I had experienced in my past, it was a process for me to let my husband touch me. I know for sure that I drove him crazy at times. But he was always so patient with me. Walt's grace was never ending with me. He always had a way of making me feel comfortable. He literally loved the hell out of me! I had to learn how to be loved properly, and he taught me that. I had to learn that it was okay to let him take the lead because he was my husband, and he always had my best interest at heart, even when I didn't understand or agree with what he chose to do. It was truly a process. It was a process that I made the choice to submit to willingly.

We rarely argued, but we had many disagreements. We both were very stubborn. I had a 2006 Mitsubishi Galant. One day Walt was out with the car, and something went wrong with the tire. Instead of just calling me to tell me what happened, he called me in an uproar! He was talking mad trash about my car and even said how he was going to leave it there. I tried to keep my composure, but he just kept going. I lashed out because he wasn't going to leave my car anywhere. I'll admit that I was wrong. I shouldn't have allowed myself to participate in his moment of frustration, but it was too late.

Once he had gotten the car back to the house, I planned to apologize first. He never gave me a chance, though. He just continued talking out of his "ass" instead of hearing and thinking about what he was saying to me. He kept saying things to see what I would say, almost trying to get a response out of me. I became upset because he questioned my love for him and even if I cared for him, strictly because I wasn't trying to feed into the already heated situation.

Not many things would make me completely tap out, but when he said what he said, I felt like a knife was stuck in my heart. He totally forgot that I shut down and get quiet when I'm upset. It wasn't because I didn't love or care for him. It was actually because I did love and care for him. I just needed some time to digress from everything. I would never blurt out anything I didn't mean in a moment of anger. I know how to shut my mouth so I won't say something I'll regret later. Walt hadn't quite mastered his part and would completely lose his top when I wouldn't respond during heated fellowship.

After that happens, I no longer want to talk. I start to build walls. *How could I be with someone who questioned my love and trust in them?* I completely shut down. There was no sex, don't look at me (naked or clothed), no touching, and no kissing either. It wasn't a kiss and makeup situation. Walt had said some hurtful things because he was upset and wasn't thinking clearly. At one point, he even mentioned that he was going to leave. I knew he wasn't going anywhere, but the fact that he allowed the situation to take him to that extreme was beyond me! I was hurting badly. I never wanted any of this to take place. If only I were given the chance to apologize.

Regardless I would have never questioned his love for me. I was stuck for a while. I didn't even sleep in our bed. Walt tried to breeze over the situation because he had settled down, but I wasn't there. I wouldn't talk because I didn't want to say anything I didn't mean.

Our apartment was right across the street from our church. We'd usually sit right beside each other. But not this Sunday. He sat in the back of the church, and I sat far away from him up the front. We were one. I could feel that he was hurting, but so was I. I had no idea how to handle this. I'm so grateful for being amid wise counsel.

Everyone knew and could see our love for each other. It just exuded. It was unusual. It was powerful and pure. Every time people saw us, they saw the glow of our love. We never had to open our mouths about it. It was unnatural for us to be distant from each other. So, the moment that we sat at different places, everyone was on it!

The musical selection began to play. It was "Let Go" by Dewayne Woods. The verse talked about not being able to fall asleep because of a vacillating mind. Though I searched for peace, I couldn't find it. My head immediately fell, and I began to weep. Everything that I was carrying, I released it at that moment. I could no longer contain it or try to be strong. I was weak. Very weak. One special person we looked up to came right up to us, pulled us aside and asked what was going on. He could tell by the looks on our faces that we were experiencing some turbulence. But he wasn't bothered. He was seasoned in his marriage, so he was aware of the turbulence. He was also confident that we'd make it through it. He didn't even need to know the details. He just told us that whatever it was, we needed to fix it now! He reminded us of our love and commitment to each other and that we'd have to fight when hard times came. He was a man of very few words, so we knew exactly what he meant. He made us hug each other after he finished talking to us. We held each other and cried in each other's arms.

We still hadn't discussed the situation, and I knew we needed to. Back when we were dating, he initiated writing letters to express ourselves and as a form of communication. That was the only way he would get anything out of me. He wrote me a letter, and I wrote him back. He asked me to come into our room, and I agreed. I didn't want to be mad at him; I missed him but was too upset to move forward. We sat on our bed, and Walt admitted his faults and apologized. His apologies were always sincere. We made up that night.

He also gave me this beautiful card.

I feel you're always with me, because I carry your
smile and your kiss in my heart wherever I go.

I feel you're always with me in the amazing ways
my life has changed because of you...

I feel you're always with me, like light,
like air, with each breath I take,
even when we're apart...

But nothing compares to really being together,
body and soul, heart to heart, in this
incredible love we share.

Miss you
With much love, ya man, ya teddy bear, Walt XOXO

On the other side of the card, he wrote:

I love you, Meka! Please 4 give me!

It's imperative to have people you and your spouse can confide in. Walt and I were young and in love, but we had much to learn about marriage. We were more than ready for the task but also open to being cultivated. We were grateful to have such amazing leaders in our lives. Our Pastor and Leading Lady Gatlin had a fruitful marriage. Walt and I looked up to them. They supported us throughout our journey. They covered, prayed, encouraged, and counseled us separately and individually. They helped us reconcile our marriage.

Our first year of marriage flew by! Our wedding anniversary was quickly approaching. I had just started working as a teacher's assistant at a daycare. Walt wanted to make our anniversary special. His job had the perks of flying for free, and he always wanted to take me places. He promised to take me around the world. He planned our anniversary trip to Miami. A few weeks before our trip, I requested that time off. Initially, my request was approved. My anniversary day was on a Monday, and my boss had decided that day would be an employee appreciation day. I explained that to Walt and asked if he was okay with me staying for that because I really wanted to be a part of that. He agreed. I came to work on the day of my anniversary. I was beyond excited! When I arrived, I was handed a note that basically said that my approval was revoked and that if I went on vacation and didn't show up for work, I would be terminated. I was crushed and confused. My boss's wife approved the initial request, and now her husband denied it. Walt and I were set to leave the next day.

How would I choose between something I loved to do and my husband? Why did I have to? I made it through work that day, and with the support of my husband, I still went with everyone for the employee appreciation day. I got all dolled up, and I sported my wedding veil. I was beaming! I wanted the world to know that I was a happy bride. That day was a celebration for me. My boss was very critical and mocked the fact that I decided to wear my veil. It didn't matter to me, though. Needless to say, my decision to travel with my husband for our anniversary was the decision that I made.

Our journey to our final destination was an adventure. Our flight went well, but Walt didn't check out how far the hotel was from the airport. I'll admit that I wasn't too happy about that. After arriving at the hotel and seeing what it looked like, I honestly didn't even want to get in the bed. I was beyond upset. I dwelled on the wrong things and made him feel like what he did wasn't good enough. That wasn't my intention, but that's how he interpreted my actions. I had to take responsibility for my actions.

The bigger picture was that Walt went out of his way to plan something special for us. Did he get everything right? NO! Was it his fault that the hotel posted one picture, and it looked like something else? NO! He tried his best. He did that all for me. I had to learn not to focus on the things that didn't matter. When I did that, I alleviated some of the unnecessary fallouts in my marriage. At the end of it all, I was so proud of my husband. He ensured that I had one hell of an experience in Miami despite the initial hiccups. It was an experience that I'll never forget.

It's important in life to cherish our loved ones. We never know when our last moment with them will be. The weeks leading up to August 5th were so special. Walt had an infectious spirit. It was hard to stay mad at him. There was never a dull moment with him, and he was rarely sad. After we got back from our vacation, everything just started to get better. One day Walt and I just sat down and talked about everything. Nothing was left on the table. When we were done talking, our relationship had such freedom. We laughed harder. We smiled bigger; it was amazing! I didn't know what was going on exactly, but I didn't care. I had no oughts with him.

We had become closer than ever before. It was the best feeling in the world! One day I was washing clothes in the basement, and Walt just came up to me, pulled me close, and started dancing! I was so confused as to what was happening. But he just kept saying babe come on and dance with me. There wasn't any music playing, but we danced around the basement. He couldn't sing at all either, but that didn't stop him from singing to me. It was like we were floating on air, without a care in the world. I was taken aback just a little because I wondered what had gotten into him. He was himself, but something was definitely different. It was a good difference, though. It was peaceful. It was joyful. It was just beautiful! I just lay in his arms after a while and let him have his way.

On the weekend of August 2nd, Walt, Tee, and I visited his mother and siblings as usual. His younger brother was taking karate classes.

Walt was more than a brother to him. He went with him to his classes that day. He had time to spend with them.

On that Sunday, I saw something miraculous with my own eyes. Walt and I knew how to pray. I don't think we ever realized how powerful we really were. Walt prayed for a member of our congregation. The Holy Spirit moved, and she fell straight to the floor. I watched his eyes get big because nothing like this had ever happened to him. I stood and watched in awe! I just wanted to know what he said to her. I saw God move that day. He showed Walt what he had inside of him. These moments were so surreal. Something was definitely happening, but what was it exactly?

TRUE LOVE

Do you know where true love lies
True love is always around and never dies
True love heals your hurts and soothes your pains
True love is shining even when it rains
His life was true, and it never ran out
He showed me what true love was all about
True love can hurt sometimes
But when the love is true, you can't stay blue for long
My husband's true love has kept me so strong

8

I'LL ALWAYS LOVE YOU

It was August 8, 2008. The day started a little bit earlier than usual. Walt had to work later, but first, he had to pay a ticket that we got on the car. While he was out, I cooked his breakfast, packed his lunch, and ironed his clothes for work. When he returned home, everything was ready for him. Walt just smiled and said, "Thanks, babe," with a big kiss and a hug. He never felt entitled to get anything. He always showed so much gratitude when I went out of my way for him. That's what made it easy for me to do things. It was an honor for me to be able to make him smile.

Walt took his job seriously. He always wanted to become better at what he did, and his goal was to make a better life for his family. His shift started a little later, but he wanted to go in a little earlier this day. We had one car, so I'd usually drop him off and pick him up from work. We got everything loaded into the car, and Walt, our daughter Tee and I started to make our way to Walt's job.

I dropped him off in Zone B. He got out, hugged, and kissed Tee. He walked to my side of the car and did the same to me. We watched him walk in, and then we headed home.

We arrived back home. Some time had gone by now. My nana lived four doors down from us, so Tee went over there. I was in the living room on the computer when I received a text from Walt that said, "I love u always." This was the norm for Walt. He'd never let a moment go by without letting me know he loved me. He would literally "I love you" me to death. I smiled and told him that I loved him too. There wasn't any more communication between us after that. It wasn't anything out of the normal, though. He was working, and I knew I'd hear from him soon.

My phone began to ring, and I didn't recognize the number. I usually don't answer unknown numbers, but this number kept calling back. When I answered, a man's voice was on the other end. He confirmed that he was speaking to me and proceeded to tell me that Walt had been in a bad accident. I immediately asked him if he was okay, but he didn't give me that answer. He responded that I needed to get to the hospital immediately. He informed me what hospital he was at. I called my nana and let her know what was going on. I asked her to keep Tee for me, and I told her that Mommy had to go to the hospital because Daddy had an accident. I let my mom know what was going on too. She just told me to keep her posted on what was going on.

Initially, I wasn't worried, panicked, or afraid. Walt was more than careful. He knew how dangerous his job was, and he took every precautionary measure needed to get back home to us. As I drove to the hospital, I began talking to God. I said, "Lord, what did he do? God, if he has lost a leg or an arm, it doesn't matter to me. I just want him to be okay." I heard the Holy Spirit say it clear as day, "I got him." I replied, "Good, well, keep him until I get there!" I had so much peace, even more now knowing that God told me He's got him. So, I know that he's going to be okay. Before getting to the hospital, I had rehearsed in my head what I would say when I fussed at him.

I pulled up to the location that the man on the phone gave me. It wasn't a hospital at all. This was the first time I panicked because I needed to get to my husband quickly. After calling the man several times and finally getting him on the phone, I discovered he had given me the wrong address. I was pretty pissed off at this point. I drove as quickly as I could to the hospital's parking lot. I walked into the hospital and asked them for my husband's room number. The receptionist told me that he didn't have a room. I was confused because I was told he was here, so where was his room? After checking the system, the receptionist told me I needed to check the ER.

I was a little overwhelmed at this point, but I made my way over to the ER. The place was packed! There were people everywhere. It was standing room only. As soon as I walked in, I walked to the first receptionist and gave her my husband's info. She couldn't give me any clear information. She told me to speak to another receptionist on the other end of the ER. I walked up to her and began to explain what was happening. I asked her where Walt was, and her look sent chills through my body. Her eyes began to well up with tears as she turned away from me. She couldn't even look at me. She informed me that Walt was a trauma patient and that a chaplain would be out to speak to me soon.

I didn't know what was happening, but at this point, I knew that it wasn't good. I called my mom back and told her what the receptionist had just told me. I said, "Mom, she said that Walt is a trauma patient" Her response was, "Oh my God, a trauma patient, that's not good." Her response confirmed my worst nightmare.

In the middle of the ER, I let out the most gruesome wail. I could no longer contain the many emotions I felt at that instant. It was so loud! Nothing or no one around me even mattered at that point. My mom was still on the phone trying to get me to talk to her, but

I couldn't formulate the words. She was working at the time and asked me if she needed to come. I still couldn't formulate the words. She knew that she had to get to me immediately. She told me she was on her way, and we hung up. I was absolutely hysterical at this point. I cried and screamed, "Where is my husband?", "I just want my husband!"

The first receptionist tried her best to console me, but I was inconsolable. This pain was unbearable. I was 22 years old, in the middle of the ER, by myself; something was wrong with my husband, and nobody told me what was happening.

An older African American woman entered the lobby and called me. With tears in my eyes, I made my way to her. She took me into a small room that was attached to the lobby. It was like a secret door that was built into the wall. I'd been in this ER before, but I'd never seen this place. We walked in, and she closed the door. She asked me to sit down, but I couldn't. She tried to get me to breathe, but I couldn't. *What was breathing anyway?* I started to hyperventilate.

Another door opened. This door was attached to the room that we were in. Two doctors appeared, and their faces looked just like the second receptionist's face did earlier. Full of gloom and despair. She looked up at me and said the most horrific words to me. She said, "Mrs. Bailey, I'm sorry, but we did all we could." At that very moment, I felt the life leave my body as I collapsed to the floor. Everyone rushed to me to try to get me in a chair.

I died that day in that room. My phone was ringing off the hook, but between the tears that blinded my sight and the air that left my lungs, I had nothing left to give. I couldn't see, nor could I talk. My mom was the first to arrive, and the news rocked her, also. However, she tried to stay strong for me.

My phone rang again, and it was Walt's mom. She wanted to know what was going on with her baby. *How could I tell her that he was gone?* I couldn't contain my tears as she yelled, "Shameka, what's going on?

Please tell me what's happening?" I had to confirm her worst nightmare. I cried out, "Walt's gone!" I'll never forget his mother's wail. It was gut-wrenching! She screamed, "No, not my baby!" I felt her pain but couldn't bear to hear her cries. I was already in shock and blacked out a few times. This could not be real. This had to be a bad dream.

All I wanted to do was see my husband. Our pastor and first lady had arrived, and after many pep talks with the doctors, I was ready to see him. Everyone couldn't go back with me. I could only take two other people with me. His parents hadn't arrived yet, so I, my mom and our pastor went to see him. As I crept around the corner, I saw him. He was lying on a gurney, covered in white sheets. He had tubes everywhere. Some were filled with blood. He had a large tube coming out of his mouth. His face was so swollen I couldn't even recognize him. His eyes were swollen shut too. I was looking at my whole heart stretched out on this table, breathless. I rubbed his head like I'd typically done and let him know I was there. As I cried out, "JESUS, JESUS, JESUS!" I had no more words. I didn't want to leave his side. He had to get up and come home.

I literally tried to unwrap him. "Where is his ring?" "Where is his stuff?" I asked them. He wore multiple armbands, but I never knew what they said. He had a yellow armband on his left arm. That was the only thing that I took off of him that day. When I started to move things around, the doctor respectfully asked me not to because of what I might see. Other than that, nobody bothered me. Everyone stood in the background as I wept over my husband's body. I felt better now that I'd seen him, but it hadn't set in yet that this was my new reality.

By the time I returned to the room, more family had arrived. There were many hugs and tears. Everyone was in disbelief. Nobody really knew what to say to me. My phone began to ring off of the hook from the news reporters. I had no clue how they got my information, but they wanted to confirm Walt's condition. As if I wasn't going through enough, these jokers were calling to get a story. I was floored, honestly. Of course, no information was given to them, and I just allowed my mom to handle my calls because I had no energy for it. I just needed to get away for a moment. I had cried so much that my tear ducts were dried out. I had nothing.

I eventually made my way into the crowded ER again. Some of Walt's coworkers had come out to see him. They asked how he was doing, and again my heart sank. I replied, "Y'all don't know?" They had no clue. Again, I had to be the bearer of bad news to more people. My heart was already broken, and now I'm getting ready to break theirs too. I told them that Walt was gone. Immediately one coworker screamed, "Noooooo," as she ran out of the ER. Another went after her while the others dropped their heads and cried in disbelief. Walt was loved by so many.

I stayed at the ER all night until they moved his body to the medical examiner's office. That walk from the ER across the bridge to the parking lot was a walk I wish I had never taken. It was quiet. The atmosphere was somber. I felt empty. As my family and I stood outside the ER, I realized what time it was. I had to go and get Walt from work. I couldn't be late. I called his phone, but there was no answer. I told them that I had to go get Walt from work. I didn't want them to tell me that Walt was not there and I couldn't go get him.

I dreaded going back home. *How was I going to tell our baby that her daddy wasn't coming home? How could I face her and break her little heart forever?* I just couldn't do it. Once my mom and I arrived at my nana's house, Tee wanted to know what was wrong with Daddy. She already knew something terrible had happened; she just didn't know what. She had a clue because while she was watching the news with my nana, though they had no confirmed news, they broadcasted that there was a bad accident at Walt's job. It didn't take long for her to put two and two together. Mommy went to the hospital because Daddy had an accident. Now it's on the news, and Mommy is here without

Daddy. My mom took her into the kitchen and tried to console her as she confirmed the news.

My world as I knew it had changed forever, but I was so shocked that it just didn't register. I went back down the street to my mother's house, and I couldn't sleep. She had pictures everywhere, and she had framed one of my favorite pictures of Walt and me. I'd sit and stare at that picture for hours while sobbing. My mom wanted me to stay with her, but I just wanted to go home. Home is where my husband was. I never really rested until I got home.

On my first day back at our apartment, I ran through the whole place. It was trash day, and Walt had to take the trash out. When I opened my apartment door, a church member was inside cleaning for me. I didn't really pay attention to her because I had to find Walt. He had to be there. I ran to our bedroom, calling his name. I ran to the kitchen, calling his name. I even ran down to the basement, looking for him. *He had to be here. We were just down here dancing together.* I continued calling out his name, but he didn't answer me back. That's the day that I realized that he was really gone.

Walt and I had lived in our apartment for a while and never had many visitors. Now there were so many people packed into my apartment that there wasn't any room left to move. *Where were all of these people when he was here?*

It was time to plan his homegoing service, and everyone wanted to be a part of the obituary as if it was some type of celebrity magazine or something. People were naming people that I'd never even heard of before. Most of them were already dead. I just didn't understand. This made no sense to me.

I'd usually spend my days in our bedroom. Nobody was allowed to come in or sit on our bed. I had to keep things how they were. Nobody even saw me walk by while they fussed about what went where. I was a zombie. Physically there, but I was gone. I hadn't eaten or slept in days. A shower was a foreign excursion, and what did I need to do my hair and get cute for anymore? I kept myself for him, his eyes only. Now that he was gone, I had no reason to. Walt was a big guy. He stood over six-feet tall and was a solid 200+ pounds. I had a pair of his pants on and another pair of his pants wrapped around my neck.

As I made my way to the front door, I'd already made peace with the fact that my family would raise our daughter. I walked right out the door, and nobody said a word. A few family members sat outside, but I walked right by them. It was crazy that nobody stopped me. I crossed the street and started walking down the next block. I walked right past one of our neighbor's houses. We didn't talk much, but my husband and I had some small chats with him, and he visited our church occasionally. When he saw me, he immediately knew that something was wrong. I wept uncontrollably and had my husband's pants wrapped around my neck. He asked me if everything was okay, and I shook my head no. I kept walking, and he began to follow me. As I approached the next block, traffic was moderate. I planned to lie in the street so someone could hit me. I did just that. I ran into the intersection and laid right down. I was lifeless and ready to go be with my husband. That's when my neighbor came running towards me, shouting in panic for me to get up out of the street. He tried to pick my limp body up, and I tried my hardest to resist. He said, "Come on, man, you can't be doing this." But I didn't care. I told him just to let me go, but he wouldn't. By this time, my phone is ringing off the hook because everyone has realized I'm gone. I never answered, though. I continued walking, and he continued following me. He kept asking me to give him my phone, but I refused. I didn't want his help. Nobody could help me. I just wanted him to leave me alone.

At this point, I was so dehydrated. My eyes were dang near swollen shut. This guy still wanted to help. We were passing a Chinese store, and he asked if I wanted some water. I replied no. He ran into the Chinese store anyway, and I tried to scurry away, but my feet wouldn't go fast enough. Before I knew it, he was right beside me again. He had brought me water, but I didn't want it. He pleaded with me to drink it, so I finally took a sip. I didn't drink much because I just couldn't. My phone continued to ring, but I still wouldn't answer. I continued to refuse to give it to him too. I didn't want anyone to find me. I didn't even want him to be following me, but he wouldn't just go away.

As I continued walking down the street, I was lifeless. I saw people's looks and stares, but I didn't care. I had no reason to live anymore. I'm sure people thought that I was crazy when they saw me. I had Walt's pants wrapped around my neck, eyes swollen shut; I had little words to say. When the guy would ask me questions, all I could do was lift my head and stare helplessly. I just kept on walking.

I planned to go to the creek and jump in. I just wanted to be with my husband, that's it. As we approached a major intersection, I watched the cars zoom by. He told me not to think about doing something crazy, so I just crossed the street without a fight. When I got to the creek, I was so fatigued. I sat on the park bench. My vision was blurred by the tears that had flooded my eyes. He sat on another bench not too far from me but far enough to give me some space. He told me that no matter what, he wasn't going to leave me. He never left my side.

I just sat there watching the traffic zoom by, entirely still in disbelief. A man on a scooter rode right by me. I saw who it was, but I wasn't interested in him finding me. After he realized that it could've been me, he doubled back. He stopped in front of the bench where I was sitting and said, "Shameka, is that you?" I had no words. I could only lift my head and gaze hopelessly into his eyes. It was my Uncle E. He gave a huge sigh of relief as tears began to fill his eyes. He told me I didn't have to do this and everything would be okay. Yet still in my mind, though, nothing would ever be okay. He initially wanted me to get on his scooter. He actually tried to usher me to it. But I fought him. He just kept saying, "Come on, Meka." I fell out on the sidewalk and sat Indian style. I couldn't go back home. I had to be with my husband. Without a second thought, I dashed towards the street. I didn't get far, though. I screamed, "Just let me go!" Suddenly a red car pulled up, and I heard voices yelling, "Who are you, and why are you touching my cousin?" The voices were my big cousins. They didn't know who my Uncle E was. But he told them who he was.

Apparently, everyone was out searching for me; meanwhile, I just wanted them to forget that I even existed. The day that my husband died, I died too. *Why didn't they get that?* They tried to get me into the car, I tried to run again, but they didn't let me get far. I sat lifeless inside of the car as they drove me back home. When I got in, everyone was relieved. My nana asked me why I didn't answer her calls. Some people said that I can't be doing stuff like that. But I didn't care. I just sat Indian style on the floor in my hallway with my head hung low. Nobody understood my pain.

I'd lock myself in our bedroom. Nobody was allowed in there. I had to keep everything just the way that it was. I didn't want anybody on my bed either. I could still smell him. His scent was everywhere. I couldn't sleep. I wouldn't eat. This was the worst pain that I'd ever experienced. I wouldn't even bathe or groom myself. I did all of that for him. I never wanted another man to look at me because I was his. My mom would come into our room and try to get me to eat. I wouldn't eat much, though.

Some time passed, and I still hadn't received his things. I wanted to know where his stuff was. I received a call from the medical examiner's office. I could finally pick up the things he had on him. A part of me was relieved, but I dreaded having to pick up his stuff from there. I received his ring and some other things, but I really was looking for his phone. His phone held so many memories of us. It would have brought me a little peace to see them. His phone wasn't there, though. I later discovered that some of his stuff was still at his job and kept for evidence. I eventually received a box from his job with his things inside, and I received his phone. It was shattered, so my hopes of retrieving anything were gone.

It was time to prepare for Walt's homegoing service. Walt had left me so many messages behind, but the one that stood out most was the yellow armband I took off his arm back in the hospital. The armband had the words "Live Strong" on it.

Before Walt's passing, I never knew what that armband said. I felt like he was speaking to me. The message was for me to "Live Strong!"

This was a message for everyone he had left behind also, so I found out where they sold the armbands, and I went and bought some for those who came out to his service.

I wanted him to be the fly guy he was, so I went out and bought him an all-white three-piece suit and a pair of shoes to match. The attire for his service was all white with hints of blue. There wasn't anything dark about Walt's life, so I didn't want anyone wearing black.

It was the final viewing the night before his service, and he looked like he was sleeping. I just talked to him and told him how handsome he was. We'd always hold hands, so I would hold his hand and squeeze it as if he could squeeze my hand back. The funeral director even jokingly reminded me that he couldn't hold my hand back. We all just laughed. I just loved him so much.

The next day was Walt's homegoing service. It was just so surreal. I had only been married to the love of my life for one year and 29 days. Eight days later, I was saying my final goodbyes. Everyone gathered at our apartment, and we took a limo to the church where his service would be held. I couldn't believe the number of people that showed up that day! It was a pretty big church, but there was standing room only.

There were literally thousands of people there. Some of whom Walt didn't even know personally. They just knew of him, or he may have just spoken to them in passing. I was in awe of the many stories that people would tell me. Nobody had a bad word to say about Walt. I was so proud of my husband. He had only been on this earth for 22 years, and he had made such an impact on people.

I stood and greeted everyone as they entered the sanctuary. They were amazed at my strength to be able to do such a thing. It wasn't any strength of my own. It came straight from Heaven! I couldn't fall apart because I was on assignment. Standing behind the podium, I began speaking to the people. Walt had lived a beautiful life. He had brought all of us together. To see him again, we must have a relationship with Jesus. At that moment, I broke. It didn't matter how many tears they shed. If Walt really meant anything to them, they needed to fall in love with the one whom Walt loved.

My mom held me as I wept and cried out for those left here alive to receive salvation. My heart felt so heavy for them. I truly believe that was my mission for that day. It was not to cry over my husband's body. He had made it to his destination. My concern at that moment was the destination of those left behind.

I made it through the rest of Walt's homegoing celebration. He was honored like the great man that he was! We had a huge repast, and the interment was private. I had his body cremated. It was so important for me to have him near me. I would've never been able to visit his gravesite. Having him home made me feel better.

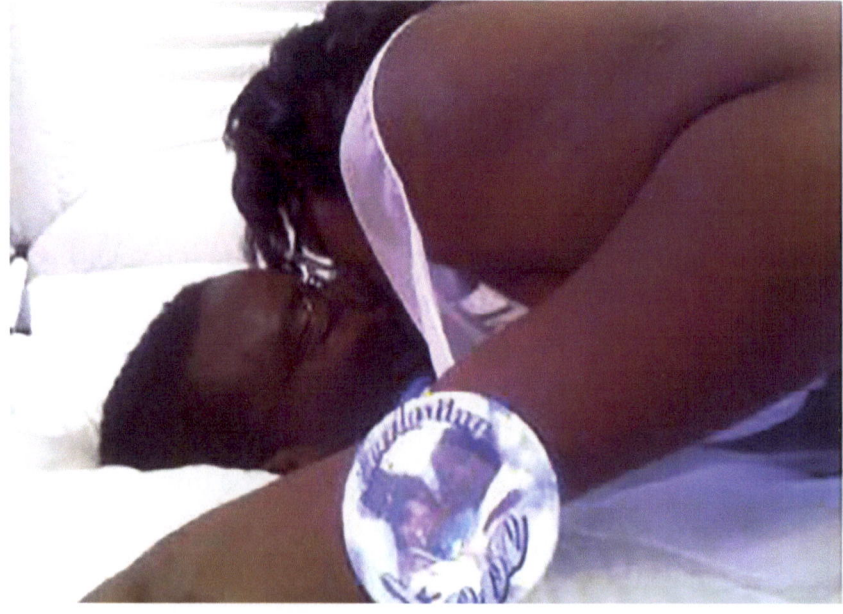

A Celebration of Life

for

Walter Martez Bailey

Destiny Began
April 27, 1986

Destiny Fulfilled
August 5, 2008

SERVICE
Wednesday, August 13, 2008
Viewing: 9:00 a.m. — Service: 11:00 a.m.

Mt. Zion Pentecostal Church of God In Christ

20th and Jefferson Streets
Philadelphia, Pennsylvania 19121

Bishop William H. Chancey, Pastor

Reverend Daniel Gatlin, Eulogist
Pastor, New Creations in Christ Church of the Way
417 South 56th Street, Philadelphia, Pennsylvania 19143

HIS LIFE STORY & SERVICE OF CELEBRATION

OUR PRECIOUS MEMORIES

HIS WORDS & HIS DESIRE & MESSAGES OF LOVE

JUST BE

My heart is broken into a million pieces
What is life
I've lost my reason
My life will never be the same
I'll never smile again
He was my best friend
I could depend on him

I've experienced a loss
Too much for my mind to comprehend
Right now, I don't need for you to find a remedy
I just need you to be a friend
They say that silence is golden
Will you just be there to hold me
As I weep
Your presence is the best gift that you can give me
So no words are necessary
Just be

9

THE IMPORTANCE
OF SUPPORT

Having the support of others was so imperative in my journey. I had crossed over into a world that I'd known nothing about. I was unwillingly thrown into a foreign land from which I couldn't escape. I was lost for so long. I'm forever grateful for those who refused to let me die, though I was ready to get out of here! After my silent escape from my house, my 71-year-old nana wouldn't leave my side. She would sleep in my living room on a futon. She wouldn't leave until she knew that I was okay. People may not always know what to say to those in their time of loss, but their presence is what's important. They can't fix it, so it doesn't matter what they say. As much as they have the mind to help, it doesn't. Our pastor and leading lady would knock on my front door until I answered. They didn't even have to come in. They stood right there in the doorway just to tell me that they loved me and were there for me. They didn't try to fix anything because they couldn't. But it was their mere presence that helped keep me. Each step of the way, they were right there to guide me along my journey. It was hard for me to do just about anything.

Walt and I did everything together. So, there wasn't a place on earth that didn't remind me of him or a moment we shared. I had a hard time going outside of my home. It hit me hard when I tried to go back to church. We ran the children's ministry together. We would work together on our lessons. We were so passionate about it. The ministry meant so much to us. I had no idea how I was going to be able to do it without him. I tried to ease my way back into service. I was used to him sitting right there beside me. I would carry his obituary and sit it in the seat next to me. It was so hard to look over and not see him there. Though the adjustment was hard, it brought me comfort. I'm grateful for the love from my church family. They let me grieve in a way that worked for me. I never felt the pressure to just get over it. That was so important in my grieving process. My mother was my greatest support system. As time passed, she was right at the forefront, helping me handle what I was up against after Walt's passing. I didn't have the strength to. The events were too traumatizing for me to sit through again. Under pressure, I would either weep uncontrollably or snap the hell out! My mom was like my interpreter and translator. When I couldn't formulate the words to express my emotions, she could. For a while, she was my mouthpiece. I'm grateful for my mother being there to stand in the gap for me.

Walt's coworkers loved him so much, and they showed it! They raised money for us and sent cards, flowers, and donations. On Friday, September 12, 2008, his coworkers put together a fish fry in memory of Walt. Though it was hard to be in the vicinity of where he worked (because that's where he took his last breath), it was comforting knowing that his coworkers' love for him extended beyond the grave.

Walt had many friends. Some were more like family. The years he put into an organization called "Freedom School" brought about lasting lifelong relationships. He was affectionately known as "Mobetta" and greatly loved.

Here's a message from one of Walt's former employers, mentors, and friends (written September 2, 2008).

Sista Shameka, I just wanted to let you know how much I admired your grace and demeanor during the services. It would have been completely acceptable for you to have said very little and interacted very little in this extremely difficult time, but you didn't. You were caring for us and showing us a bright and hopeful face, and for that, I thank you so much. I also want to encourage you to feel entirely free to boohoo, cry, rant, and scream if you need to. There is no shame in it. That's all a part of it. Don't feel that you have to continue to be the strongest person in the room. Sorrow is able to pass when you give it time to flow.

Unfortunately, I have had some very close deaths to me, and I genuinely thought they would be the end of me, but I found that being able to come out of the sadness whole depended on my willingness to fully experience the depths of what I was experiencing. There will never be a time when you don't miss him, but eventually, missing him will not hurt as badly. I am praying for you and your family, and although I did not answer the altar call, I want you to know that I saw God in Walter, and he helped me to be a stronger, more spiritual person.

You are beautiful and powerful, and I give thanks for you. Give me a call if you need anything.

Here's a message dated October 8, 2008:

> *Hey, Meka boo, I feel like crying sometimes too. I know that you're a strong woman, and you will hold ya head up high for u and Tee. I read the comments on his page all the time…. some songs I hear makes me think of him…man do I miss my brother. I replay the memories in my head over and over…I just want it to be a dream. Everybody asks me if I am ok. I always say yea, when the truth is I miss everybody sooo much, and I can hear Walt tellin me not to work too much, lolol. But we will get thru this. I will pray for you, and I love you.*
>
> *Look what Walt has done. He has brought everybody together, which probably wouldn't have happened in the midst of our sometimes too-busy lives. He has made us "Mo Betta," lol.*

Looking back at these messages brought tears to my eyes. At what was supposed to be the weakest time in my life, hell, I even felt weak; people say they saw strength! I can't take any credit for that. That was only GOD! He truly kept me! Walt had transitioned, and across the board, everyone saw God in him. Everyone acknowledged that whatever connection he had with him, he made them better. That's what we are supposed to do. The goal of our lives is to live a life so others might ask what must they do to be saved. Our lives should draw others to God. Walt's life did just that, and he surpassed that goal.

Support also poured out from Walt's former classmates, people from his past, and whoever knew of Walt. I'd have so many people I've never met contact me on social media and express their condolences.

A year after Walt's death, I organized a "Celebration of Life" party in Walt's memory. I wanted to gather those who meant the most to

Walt and just remember him. We played games; we laughed and cried. We shared our fondest memories. We wrote personal messages on some heart and star-shaped balloons and released them to fly up to Heaven. I created a special video arrangement to Keyshia Cole's song "Sent from Heaven." There was no other way to describe Walt. He was "HEAVENSENT." It was full of our most precious memories. Walt has some amazing friends! Some of which I've been able to build my own bond with to this day.

Each step of the way, God placed people in my life to help guide me through. As time passed, God was intentional about the people he used to support me when I needed them. There are too many to name, and they know who they are. I just want to say "Thank You" for every phone call, text, hug, encouraging word, prayer, the time you took to get me out of the house, every listening ear and shoulder I had to cry on, etc. Your love was everything that I needed to keep me when I didn't know how to be kept. I appreciate you all!

WHERE DO I GO NOW?

Where do I go now
I feel like I'm drowning
In a river of my own tears
I need someone to save me
From this bad dream
Am I really awake
My world has been rocked like an earthquake
Will I ever recover
My best friend, my homie, my lover
Went from laying right next to me
To a lifetime memory

Where do I go now
When I need to escape
From my new reality
I don't want to accept this
Is there a reject
Button somewhere
Because this is not how I wrote my story
I can't comprehend how a love like mine had
to end
In tragedy
I'm shattered, you see
Sometimes I don't know whether I'm coming or
going
Sometimes company helps
Other times I just want to be alone
I feel so wrong for still being here
Without you
What am I to do now

10

HOW CAN I LIVE WITHOUT YOU?

Steps To Healing: The Grieving Process

How can I live without you? Those thoughts would always flood my mind. We were just beginning to create our lives together. Everything that we did, we did it together. Walt took on a lot of responsibilities, some things I just didn't have to do. Now that he's not here, I have to do everything. In a moment, my whole world was changed forever.

Grieving is an entire process. You can't go around it. You have to go through it. There are several steps in this process. You'll try to bargain with God. You'll feel shocked, disbelief, denial, guilt, anger, depression, sadness, acceptance, and hope. These feelings will occur in no particular order, but please know you'll feel them all! The key is to acknowledge where you are, accept it, and feel that emotion at that moment. You must go through every step. The moment that you start to try to skip steps, you'll thwart your healing process. I guarantee you that you won't heal properly. This process is uncomfortable. Again there is no particular order. Your stage is subject to change quickly, and that's perfectly fine! Embrace where you are; your feelings are real and valid. Let nobody rush your process. There is no time limit or expiration date on your process either. It's not your job to make people understand your pain. Try to surround yourself with people who will walk with you through your process, someone whose presence will constantly remind you that you can't give up! Though we are allowed to feel and have our moments, sis, it's not okay to get stuck there! Take your moment. It's okay to sit there for a minute, but don't lie down there. Your husband would want you to live!

In the beginning, for me, I felt everything at once! When I got the news in the hospital, I was in shock, disbelief, and denial. There was no way that my husband was gone. Someone must've gotten me mixed up with someone else because my husband was at work. It wasn't until I saw him with my own eyes, lifeless on that gurney, that reality hit me. However, it hadn't really set in yet. I began to bargain with God. *God, just let my husband get up off of this table and come home because I need him here with me.* I felt a sadness that words couldn't express. Even after seeing my husband, I was still ready to go and pick him up from work. I was in denial that he was gone. I couldn't think rationally. My mind didn't have the capacity to hold all of the information that I was given. Though I physically knew what was happening, mentally, I hadn't digested what was going on. My normal routines were still supposed to happen in my mind.

When I got back to our daughter, guilt hit me like a ton of bricks. It was my fault that she lost her father. There was something that I should've seen or been able to do to prevent this from happening. I felt so responsible for her grief. I didn't know how to mother her properly for a long time. Every time I looked at her, I saw him. I saw her pain. I had to wipe her tears, and I had no words to comfort her because I couldn't comfort myself. Our baby couldn't even make it through the school day without calling me weeping. I found myself in a space that had no definition.

Reality didn't hit me in full force until I came back home to our apartment. I was in so much denial that I literally ran through our apartment, calling his name and looking for him. I was 100% sure he was there, and this was just a bad dream. I really thought his absence was temporary and that he would come walking through that door at any moment.

I felt angry with God. I'd yell and scream at the top of my lungs. Some days I'd scream and cry into my pillow. I'd question God. Why would He allow this to happen? Everything was perfect at that time in our lives. *God, everything was getting better. Why would you give me something this good and then take it away? Why me? Why my husband? Why our family?* I felt like I was being punished. The things that had transpired just didn't make any sense. We didn't deserve this. We loved God. Our lives were anchored in Him. So why did He allow this to happen to us? He could've chosen anyone else. Walt wasn't into bad things. He never got into trouble. He was a good guy. God could've chosen someone else. He could've stopped the accident. He could've saved Walt. He could've healed him. He didn't have to die!

I had no rap for God. He clearly didn't love me. He robbed me of the best thing that had ever happened to me, my husband, and he robbed my daughter of the experience of her father. *How could some-one who claimed to love me just sit back and not do anything about it? Why did He let my husband die?!?!*

I found myself telling God that He didn't care about me. As much as I wanted to punch my hands through the walls, I couldn't. I'd attack my bed, assaulting my pillows, trying to find some relief. But it was all temporary. After a while, I had completely tapped out. I was in a major state of shock. I went from this outgoing social butterfly to a flower whose life had withered away. I became mute. There were no words. My needs could only be interpreted through the pain that was seen through my eyes.

Depression crept in. I felt like a rain cloud was hovering over me, and it just wouldn't stop raining. I felt empty, I felt lonely, and I began to isolate myself. I couldn't sleep, and I had no appetite whatsoever. I went days, if not weeks, without food. I was utterly drained, and I had no energy. My feelings of sadness were never-ending. It was a garment that I had acquired and never took off. It was embedded in my skin. Wherever I was, it was there too. I couldn't escape it, so I'd waddle in it. There seemed to be no end in sight. I found comfort in leaving everything just like it was when he was here. His things were still in our drawers. His side of the dresser still had his things in it. I didn't change a thing. My living room turned into a huge memorial. Pictures of him, Tee, and I were all over the place. After a while, my mom grew concerned about that part of my grieving. She thought that I was beginning to create a shrine. I know that she meant well, but having that space brought me peace. Anything that made me feel his presence or brought him closer to me made me feel better.

When his urn arrived, I was so happy. Though it was hard to comprehend how they were able to get his six-foot 200+ pound body into this small urn, it felt good to hold him in my arms again. Some days, I would sleep with his urn next to me. I'd tuck him into bed. I'd talk to him and tell him how much he was loved and missed. Some days I'd just hold him and cry. No matter how many days went by, it was just so unreal! The fact that he wasn't physically here with me.

As much as I wanted Walt here with me, it would've been selfish. He would've been a vegetable if he had survived the accident with the extent of his injuries. He wouldn't have been the vibrant, bubbly Walt. He wouldn't have been able to take care of himself. I would've probably had to become his full-time caretaker. Taking on that responsibility and rearing our daughter might have been an enormous responsibility. It was one that I would've been willing to take!

But how would I have really felt seeing my husband in such a helpless state? As much as it hurt to be here without him, seeing him like that would hurt even more. He wouldn't have been able to be an engaged father like he once was. He would've been in constant pain. Again, it would've been selfish of me to try to keep him here.

Yes, God could've healed him. But He didn't. I found peace in knowing that Walt was in the only place that he'd rather be if he couldn't be with me. He was in the arms of his Father. The One that he always talked about. The One that he loved and adored. The One that he lived for. Walt earned his crown!

Some say that time makes things easier; I don't believe that's the case. Christ makes things easier! After almost 15 years, if I wasn't careful, I could still have a mental breakdown. Without a second thought, I would just tap out. Time hasn't taken the sting out of the tragedy of my husband's death. Honestly, sometimes the time that has gone by causes me to be reminded of what I had and what I've lost. I reminisce on how things used to be and ponder the thought of what they would've been. If I'm not careful, I will find myself in an isolated and depressed state. I should have completely lost my mind! But God has been a keeper, and He allows me to have my moments, but I can't stay there.

The truth is that grief never ends, but it changes. The memories of Walt will never go away. The magnitude of the effect of his death won't ever go away. How much I miss him will never change. Though the way that I grieve doesn't look exactly like it looked 15 years ago, I still grieve.

I still have my moments, and that's perfectly fine. I can now identify my moments and notice my triggers and when they'll come. Birthdays, holidays, or sometimes something random will trigger me. There are times when I handle it alone, and there are times when I reach out for help.

It is important not to try to "figure it out." You won't be able to wrap your mind around the events that have taken place. You'll drive yourself crazy trying to figure out what you could have or should have done. It isn't your fault. There's absolutely nothing that you could have done to stop or change it. So please don't beat yourself up about it.

No signs said, "Shameka, don't let Walt go to work because he won't make it home." There weren't any hints that my last kiss was my last kiss. When he texted me, "I'll love you always," at the time, I didn't put much emphasis on the word "always," but there was a huge significance after I found out that he was gone. He unknowingly was reminding me of his love for me and that it will always last. It was like a farewell without either of us knowing what was ahead.

The key to my healing is JESUS! I would not have made it this far without Him. He has been my mind regulator. He has been my rock. The sweet Holy Spirit has been my comforter. Though I'll never understand, God has never failed me!

There is a manual for just about everything. But there's no manual for how to live after you've honored the till death do us part portion of your wedding vows. It may seem impossible in the beginning. It won't be easy, and it won't feel good. But it is possible! I'm a living witness that there is light at the end of the tunnel. You will get your joy back, and God's peace will surpass your understanding if you allow it to. I never thought that I would be able to smile again, but I have! In JESUS' name, you will too!

I'LL NEVER FORGET

I'll never forget how you came into my world
And helped me to find my identity
You were never after what I had
You were always a friend to me

I'll never forget how you calmed my fears and soothed my pains
Your love showed me how to live again

I'll never forget your warm hugs and your sweet kisses
Your infectious laugh
Just some of the things that I'm missing

I'll never forget how you protected me
And the fact that you never neglected me
I'll never forget how you'd graciously get me in order
I'll never forget how much you loved our daughter

Your presence in my life was a gift from up above
Orchestrated by God Himself
Sent down on earth to show me His love
I'll never forget how you changed my life

I'll never forget the moment that you
asked me to be your wife
So many memories that I'll cherish forever
Because of you, my life is better

11

PRECIOUS MEMORIES

Till Death Did We Part

God used Walt to make me the happiest woman alive! He showed me His love through Walt. He showed me what love was. Something that I'd never experienced before from a man. Because of him, I can hold myself in the highest esteem. I've learned to love myself. He was the best friend, father, and husband in the world! My tough exterior didn't threaten him. He tore every wall down! He loved the "HELL" out of me. He pulled out the beauty hidden inside behind all the pain and hurt from my past. He held me when I cried and dried every tear. He proved his undying love for me by choosing me and making me his wife; for that, I'll forever cherish him.

I'LL FOREVER CHERISH

I'll forever cherish the man that God used to set me free
I'll forever cherish the man who realigned
me on the path to my destiny
I'll forever cherish the man who made my house a home
I'll forever cherish the man who never left me alone
I'll forever cherish the man who looked past my imperfections
I'll forever cherish the man who always pulled out the best in me
My husband, my lover, my friend
Till death do us part
But it's still not the end
A love that lives beyond the grave
I'll forever cherish this love for the rest of my days
I'll love you always
Forever in my heart
I'll forever cherish you

I'm forever grateful to God that He made sure that we had a clean slate before Walt departed from this earth. I live today with no regrets. Some people aren't as fortunate as I am. Their husbands left this world, and they never had that chance to reconcile. So, they carry the burden of guilt with them. I pray that you'd take it from me when I tell you that no disagreement, no heated fellowship, no miscommunication, absolutely nothing is worth holding onto. Fix it as soon as you can! We can't continue harboring things against our spouses and thinking that we will have tomorrow to fix it. The Bible tells us in James 4:14 that life is nothing but a vapor. Here one moment, and then it vanishes.

There's not always a warning sign. You can't always be prepared for death when it abruptly happens. Don't take time for granted. Cherish your spouse even in their mess. Because once they close their eyes, there are no more opportunities to get it right. They can't see your tears or hear you say I'm sorry. If you're anything like me, you'll realize that none of that stuff was worth it by that time. You'll plead with God for one more chance to speak to them. Please don't let this be you. Love your spouse to the point that you'll have no regrets when they leave here! Their death will still sting. The pain of it will be inevitable. You'll smile, knowing that you intentionally decided to fight like hell to love your spouse. It will be one of the best feelings in the world!

Walt was the most selfless person. He would give until he was completely empty. His smile radiated the whole room, and his presence commanded the room. He was a compassionate and loving husband. He was an amazing father. He was an honorable son. He was a magnificent friend. He was my confidant, my partner in crime. The ying to my yang. He was my everything. There's not a day that I don't think of him. Without having experienced his genuine love for me, I wouldn't be the woman I am today. I live my life with integrity, and I'll never settle knowing that I deserve nothing less than God's best.

Walt left me with so many memories. My most precious gifts are our children. I have pieces of him. I have the honor of raising his legacy. Our oldest Tee is a replica of him. She emulates how he loved on me and showered me with his love, random gifts, surprises, and things to show me that I'm loved. She took on his sneaker fetish. She has hundreds of them! I couldn't get her to wear a pair of shoes if I paid her to! She was his shadow, always attached to his hip. We can sit back, laugh, and cry as we reflect on the memory of him.

Our youngest, Brooke, our miracle baby, never got to experience him. But she's so much like him! Brooke is so affectionate. Her father would say I love you a million times a day; she does the same. She draws and is great at math, just like he was. She can read 20 chapter books in a day! She's the only kid I know that doesn't need help with homework! She's an adventurous eater (she will try anything, just like him). Her personality is like a magnet; everybody loves her! Before Walt passed away, he wanted to be a music producer. His newfound love was music. Both of our girls are dancing machines. They are constant reminders of him in their own ways. Even in this tragedy, I thank God for not leaving me empty-handed.

I miss how Walt used to get me together in the sweetest way. As my relationship with God grew stronger, certain songs would just take me to the throne. I'd immediately be stopped in my tracks and begin to worship and cry like a baby. My mother would jokingly say, "Oh, she's getting saved again." My trigger song was "Yes" by Shekinah Glory. Once he caught on to that, he'd used it against me. I couldn't keep an attitude with him. He'd play the song whenever he saw me getting an attitude. I'd stop right in my tracks. He didn't play fair at all, lol. Once, we were under the subway waiting for the train, and I tried to have an attitude. He turned the song on, and I tried to run away from him. I told him that he wasn't playing fair. Eventually, he made the song my ringtone.

Walt would get me the best cards. It was like he wrote the words himself. They would perfectly express how he felt about me. When he couldn't find a card, he'd make one. He'd illustrate it himself and put the sweetest words on the inside. I can read his cards today and still feel his love through them. Here are a few of my favorite cards:

YOU'RE THE ONE

The thing about you is, you're fun.
You make me laugh.
You make me feel more alive.
And, okay, you make me
a little crazy sometimes.
But there are these moments in my mind,
crystal clear images
of you and me
and how we fit together,
and it all makes such perfect
sense, and I know what I want.
I want time with you.
I want to hear you whisper
and talk and yell.
I want to touch you so softly
it puts you to sleep.
I want to fall in love so deeply with you
that, even when it's not fun at all,
I can look at you
as I do now and say,
as I do now,
"Yes, you're the one."
Happy Birthday
No words could better describe my
feelings for you! I love you, Meka!!
Enjoy ya day! Love Walt

For some special reason, Walt began to call me "Star." His cards would reflect those sentiments, and he even bought me a pair of star-shaped Swarovski earrings. This has so much more significance now! My license plate is Hisstar.

Let me show you
Just how much I love you
Let me give you
Something wonderful to remember
As I help you forget your cares
Just relax your mind
And let me soothe you
And make you understand
How important you are to me
How loved you are by me
Let me comfort you
And smooth every trace of stress
From your day
Let's surrender to the chemistry
We cannot ignore
And savor the magic
We make together
Here and now
Let me take you
In my arms
And show you
Just how very much
You're loved

On the inside of the card, he wrote, "I ♥ U!
Thank you so much for taking this journey called
"Love" with me!! I love you, Meka!!
-Ya hubby Walt

This handwritten card is my favorite!

The front of the card says:

To My Superstar

The inside reads:

Star: a celestial body of heat that requested
energy from the inside out
Shameka Michele Bailey
The brightest light ever seen by Walter Bailey.

I don't just call you that to make you smile. Truth is, your
light is the brightest to shine on me since I laid eyes on
you. Whether it's your charming smile, warm hugs, or
tender kiss that cheers me up, nothing makes me smile
more than knowing that I caught my shining star!!
Happy Mother's Day
Boo!!
Love ya hubby

Star - a celestial body of heat that radiates energy from the inside out

2.) Shameka Michele Bailey the brightest light ever seen by Walter Bailey

I don't just call you that to make you smile. Truth is, your light is the brightest to shine on me since I laid eyes on you. Whether its your charming smile, warm hugs or tender kiss that cheers me up, nothing makes me smile more than knowing that I caught my shining star!!

Happy Mother's Day Boo!!

Love, yo hubby

On our wedding day, Walt and I were supposed to recite our own vows. There was so much going on with the wedding that we just decided to do whatever was necessary to get it over with and get away. After Walt passed, I was going through some of his things, trying to salvage precious memories, and I came across a notebook. Written in his notebook were his wedding vows to me. It was like he left me a note reminding me how much he loved me.

My Vows To Meka,

I looked up the meaning of the word "blessed." It means "fully satisfied," so that means that I am blessed with you. Because for the first time, I can say that I'm truly happy and content in a relationship. We hid nothing from each other, we have chemistry, and I no longer feel stress. If just the slightest bit overcomes me, you remove it quick. I just want to let you know that I'm forever thankful that you gave me a second chance and that I'm blessed every time I wake up with you in my arms. I Love You! Those three words have my life in them. Some men say that they have seen angels. Well, I've seen you. And that's enough!

I have so many memories -beautiful, long-lasting, lifelong, precious memories that I'll cherish forever in my heart. I'll never know why God chose me. But I can say that I'm beyond honored to be Walt's wife. I'm honored to mother his legacy. I'm honored to be a beacon of light and hope to all who read our story.

It was very hard birthing this book. I had to go back and physically relive the most traumatic and happiest times of my life. All of my memories of Walt bring smiles and tears to my eyes because they are just memories now. However, I'm forever grateful to God for every one of them. I pray this book will give you a glimpse of God's love for us. If you were like me, you were neglected, violated, counted out, a teen mom, felt alone, lost, unworthy, etc. Our Father CANCELED every lie! He loved us enough to bless us with husbands made after his own heart. He allowed us to experience His love through them. May the peace of God comfort your hearts, knowing that he's safe in his Father's arms. Continue to "Live Strong!" Just as your husband would want you to.

A PRAYER FOR YOU

Father, You are an AMAZING GOD! Father, there is none like You. Father, You control the seas, and storms stop at your command. Father, all power is in Your hand. Father God, You are matchless, merciful, forgiving, and compassionate. Father God, I thank You for allowing my sister to see another day. A NEW day. A day full of PROMISE. Father God, I thank You for being a keeper. I thank You for keeping my sister through every trial and tribulation just to get her to this day. I thank You for how You're going to use her in a MIGHTY way!

Father, You are LOVE. Lord, because of You, we can truly experience TRUE love.

Father, Your word says that we overcome by the power of the blood and the word of our testimony (Revelations 12:11).

Father, I thank You for giving me a testimony that can help my sister overcome.

Father, I thank You for the life of my sister. Father, I thank You for her healing. Father, I thank You for giving her an example through me of how we can LIVE after the death of our husbands. Father, thank You for understanding where she is and how she feels and loving her enough not to leave her there.

Sweet Holy Spirit, I thank You for comforting her in the midnight hour. I thank You for being the interpreter of her tears. Father, on this day, I thank You for changing her garments! I thank You for giving her a garment of praise for her sadness. Father, please show her the beauty in her ashes. Lord, You make ALL things BEAUTIFUL! Father, it takes a certain individual to handle this journey. Father God, many would not have been able to survive what we've experienced and had to live through. Father, You saw fit for us to embark on this journey. Father, we will never understand why, but Father God, we declare today that we will continue to TRUST You!

Your ways are not our ways, and Your thoughts are not our thoughts. One thing that we can rest assured of is that ALL THINGS WORK TOGETHER FOR OUR GOOD! Father, continue to cover and keep my sister. Restore her JOY, Lord, and give her a new song. Father God, show her the purpose of her pain so that she can LIVE THROUGH IT!

In the mighty name of JESUS, I pray, Amen. ♥